Parents on Parenting

Parents on Parenting
Authentic images of parenting by those who've been there

Edited by

Barbara Cherem
and
Natalie Gianetti

Spring Arbor College Press
Spring Arbor, MI 49283

ISBN 0-9634232-0-7

To my children, Mariah and Max, who continue to be my joyful and loving teachers, and to my husband, Gabe, who continues to give us all his love and support.

Barbara Cherem

To my children, Gregory, Michelle, Douglas, Rick and Nathan; my stepdaughter, Elise; and my husband, Michael, for years of rich experiences and memories.

Natalie Gianetti

Being a good parent isn't living in fear of making mistakes; it's having faith in my power to recover from whatever mistakes I'm bound to make and moving on from there.

—Carl Pickhardt,
Parenting the Adolescent

Contents

Preface

This book provides writings by adults on family life. It captures adults being honest about what they actually learned by being parents. They all studied at Spring Arbor College from 1985–1989 in the Management of Human Resources (MHR) program. These adult students were all completing their B.A. degrees long after the age at which persons typically complete their B.A. (thirty-seven years average age).

Many colleges and universities across the United States award credit for prior learning. The Council for Adult and Experiential Learning (CAEL) has established a system by which colleges can assist students in documenting prior learning by using a model. At Spring Arbor College (SAC), David Kolb's model is used to document such learning.

All students in the MHR program learn Kolb's model and write at least one paper according to the model (see Appendices A and B). Students who have sixty transferable credits from an accredited institution and will study with SAC for thirty-four more hours may also earn up to thirty credits through this prior learning documentation process. Such students choose to submit papers prepared according to Kolb's model to a faculty reader in the discipline in which they are petitioning for credit. Faculty decide whether such experiential learning papers do indeed document prior learning equivalent to a class in their discipline. Though students can receive thirty credits in this manner, the typical number of credits earned through prior learning assessment is seventeen.

As a faculty reader from 1983–1987, Barb Cherem was struck by the unique perspectives and wealth of knowledge contained in student life learning papers. She was also struck by the depth of feeling often conveyed in the papers. She began asking students to release a copy for her later use. At that time, these papers were perceived as "treasures," but for what end no one quite knew.

As Director of the Assessment Center for Prior Learning, Natalie Gianetti read even more life learning papers as she screened student's entire portfolios prior to portions going to faculty readers. When Barb approached Natalie about using some of the "treasures" she had read, Natalie was enthusiastic about a collaborative venture. The idea of a book on parenting evolved in 1988. Since practical and honest concepts concerning nurturing, disciplining, and rearing children to adulthood are not in abundant supply, the authors wanted to share them with a wider audience. The book was finally completed in 1992.

This book can be used by colleges who use Kolb's model as a means for students to document prior learning. Though there are some papers here with only partial examples of Kolb's model, most have cycled through all four parts. While the quality of implementing Kolb's model is varied, this book provides those learning how to construct a life learning paper concrete examples. It puts "meat" on what otherwise students might perceive as an abstract and difficult model.

This book then is a selection of essays about parenting written according to Kolb's model by adults who are parents. We have tried to provide authentic images of the real-life struggles of parents who have learned something worth sharing.

The students' words are in regular type; the words of the two editors are in italics.

Acknowledgements

We would like to acknowledge the many adult students who have labored over life learning papers, especially those whose papers we ended up using in this parenting volume. Their struggles and insights are a continuing source of inspiration.

Thanks to Jane Rieder who helped in final editing, and to Amy Philson and Brenda Loucks who typed careful and repeated drafts over a lengthy time. Thanks particularly to Brenda for her helpfulness and spirited involvement in whatever she works on. Thanks also to Wally Metts for his expertise in publishing, which enabled this Spring Arbor College publication.

Lastly, thanks to Vice-President of Marketing George Kline for his enthusiasm, encouragement and partial financial backing of our belief that knowledge gained through experience is worth sharing with a wider public.

Barbara Cherem
Associate Professor, Education

Natalie Gianetti
Dean for Alternative Education

Contributors

Eldon Abraham from Clarkston, Michigan
Evelyn Bacon from Jackson, Michigan
Fred and Linda Browning from Columbia, Tennessee
Jonas Castro from Holt, Michigan
Cherry Joseph from Flint, Michigan
Linda Haas from Seattle, Washington
James Lowe from Toledo, Ohio
Stephanie McLaurine-Hughes from Lansing, Michigan
Barb Oliver from Jackson, Michigan
Floyd Ramseyer from Fostoria, Michigan
Raymond Slumpff from Belleville, Michigan
Gregory Rodriguez from Burton, Michigan
Vivian Rogers from Livonia, Michigan
Linda Smith from Wixom, Michigan
Jean Taylor from Dearborn, Michigan
plus those that asked to remain anonymous

Introduction

Authentic Images of Parenting

Images control us. They're potent. They're what we measure ourselves against . . . from the ideal "nuclear family" to the ideal nurturing parent.

In a time in America when small towns were common, when there was a rich community life, people recognized falsity. They also granted acceptance. It was difficult in such a context to be sold false images; everyone knew many people and their families. Even if others tried to sell a false image, people knew inauthentic images when they saw them and they learned to accept the imperfection of authentic people. That horrendous woman who could snub and gossip could also be a person of unlimited dedication to the church. She could deliver a children's sermon that inspired and direct a bell choir of adolescents with whom nobody else would work. It was not hypocrisy; it was the complexity of real people—spiritual, physical, intellectual, emotional people.

Where then do we get our images of how to be an effective parent, especially if our own family hasn't provided what we'd like to give our own children? Experience is often the teacher, albeit a slow and cumbersome one. Sometimes we look to others' experience, perhaps avoiding some of our own trial-and-error learning. Some families look to television's images. However, this book is an attempt to learn through others' experiences, through authentic images of parenting, rather than what we might subtly receive through the television images of the "Cosby Show," "Full House" or "Roseanne."

The adult students' stories are a bit like Eliot Wigginton's Foxfire series in which his adolescent students documented the folklore and folkways of Appalachia. Here were undiscovered treasures, overlooked merely because they were common and close at hand. This method of documentation was simply his attempt to involve uninvolved students in the life near at hand, yet it yielded a social movement in education as well as nine Foxfire books, a television station and an historic village.

Similarly, the first-hand knowledge parents have learned becomes "common sense," some of which has become increasingly uncommon. This book is an opportunity to share some wisdom of what it means to be a parent in modern America. A book written by parents for parents, it's also a book written for family ecologists and family life educators. It can be used by college instructors as a book of readings which supplements more theoretical and academic textbooks in human development. Additionally, it illustrates Kolb's model for colleges who teach students this manner of documenting prior learning. It is a book constructed from life learning papers of adult students who are parents. There were many wonderfully inspiring papers; we are only sorry that we could only select a few.

Many false, media-influenced images of family life prevail today. By trying to live up to such perfect or false images, we create a superficiality and emptiness that are both dishonest and stressful. On a recent sitcom, the single teen mom at her baby's delivery is surrounded by flowers, an expensive negligee, and her friends, yet is estranged from her parents. She dials them up and easily reconciles with them. In real life such ease and support do not surround the baby born out of wedlock. Terms like "single teen mom" may help soften the harsh reality, but they sometimes join with television's false images to present an image that inexperienced teens actually believe. Any false images which aren't perceived as comedy, such as the false ("Roseanne") and the perfect ("Cosby"), are equally grotesque, perhaps more dangerous than the more overt fantasies of pornography. Such images contribute to dissatisfaction with self, children, and, ultimately, marriage and family life.

Through presenting some honest stories of the struggles and joys of parents, we hope we have contributed to an unmasking of false images of family life. These examples are diverse and complex, yet all are filled with an authenticity and richness we can look at and admire. These are real people with real problems.

May you enjoy their insights as we have.

Chapter One

Balanced discipline for smooth sailing

Barbara Cherem

Of the hundreds of life learning papers I've read on parenting over the past six years, discipline is easily the most frequently selected topic. Whether permissive, authoritarian, or authoritative, parents struggle to find an appropriate balance point: Will physical punishment tame a wildly unconventional child into a solid citizen? Or will allowing children to express themselves as individuals stimulate a natural goodwill and solid citizenship? These parents demonstrate how they each attempt to negotiate a harmonious position in their own families. Each has quite different disciplining techniques. The balance point is as variable as the parents' backgrounds and experiences.

Adults and children coexisting in the same boat soon learn that to become a community called a family, they must solve the discipline dilemma. The family either tumultuously heaves and rocks through high waves, enough to cause sea sickness, or else it sails smoothly along. Much of this rough or smooth sailing depends on the appropriate balance of its keel, discipline. Building family community through building a sense of family membership may well be discipline's most important societal contribution.

The child psychologist Bruno Bettelheim provides an ancient definition of discipline:

The original definition of the word discipline refers to an instruction to be imparted to disciples . . . Acquiring discipline and being a disciple are intimately related . . . [The disciples'] deepest wish was to emulate Christ. They made him their guide not just because they believed in his teachings but because of their love for him and his love for them. Without such mutual love, the master's teaching and example, convincing as they were, would never have persuaded the disciples to change their lives and beliefs as radically as they did. The story of Christ's disciples suggests that love and admiration are powerful motives for adopting a person's values and ideas.[1]

Love is apparent in each of the three parents who share their parenting experiences and learning in this chapter. Parents are seen as loving guides hoping to be modeled by loving children. Some children are reluctant disciples, while some parents are reluctant leaders. Barbara Oehlberg makes parents aware that building children's self-discipline and cooperation takes both patience and noise:

Parents and teachers cannot *make* children engage in constructive behavior. In fact, we cannot make them *do* anything. But through creative communicative skills, we *can* generate the motivation by which our children may *choose* to engage in cooperation and extend compassion to others.

The key is language. We can nurture trust that words can and do work by permitting children to work through their conflicts—even though this may be a lengthy and noisy process. Parents may need to lovingly contain or stop certain physical actions, but we must be careful not to do the children's "work" for them. By asking questions instead of giving solutions or demands we can guide our children's thinking toward alternative choices or solutions. Our goal is not to change our children's feelings but to help them recognize alternative behaviors.[2]

Parental questioning and negotiation are exemplified in the following stories. As these parents adjust and readjust the keel in their family life, we observe how much patience and awareness this parenting task takes.

Responding to changing needs: a father's discovery

In this section a father writes about establishing discipline for his young daughter, Joy, when he returns from the military. The dad describes his own reevaluation of suitable boundaries as they relate to his discipline methods. The movement from an external source of authority to a more internalized voice for the child later results in a more self-disciplined teenager.

Grounding a Child's Security

In the scriptures, discipline is clearly presented as an obligation of a parent: "Whom the Lord loves He reproves, even as a father the son in whom he delights."[3] It is an integral part of training. Even more importantly, it is as much a part of love as more "positive" displays of that love. A parent must learn to use and administer discipline in a positive and loving manner to fulfill his obligation in rearing and nurturing his child. Most of the learning depicted in this section involves the oldest child, our daughter Joy. Unfortunately, the oldest child is generally the test case as the parents learn to do their job. Fortunately, the worst experimentation is done early enough that the child does not remember the parents' gross early failings.

Concrete Experience

During most of the first two years of Joy's life, I was gone with the military. Sue, in her own words, tried to treat Joy as a small adult, as a friend rather than as a child. Instead of disciplining Joy, Sue tried to reason with her and implore her toward good behavior. As a consequence, when I returned from overseas, Joy was a "brat." She was exceedingly strong-willed and undisciplined. She was accustomed to doing as she pleased and was unwilling to follow directions, frequently to her detriment.

Reflective Observation

Some of the observations about the situation were clear and obvious; others, however, were more subtle and took some time to discern. Clearly, a parent's treating his child as a friend negates the authority that the parent has available to exercise in training the child. If the child is treated as a friend, then, like a friend, the child expects a measure of autonomy. It becomes apparent that treating a child as a small adult is not good for the child or the relationship. There are no common values, and therefore no possibility of the child's responding in the manner expected by the parent. The last observation took some time to occur to me because I knew nothing of two-year-old children or of my own daughter because I had not been with her for two years. Joy was very insecure and, in spite of her outward forcefulness, could not cope with circumstances around her.

Abstract Concepts

Children need discipline to deal with the world around them, to mature, to learn and to be trained in the things that are appropriate to their level. To whatever extent this discipline is denied and those steps are not accomplished, the foundation for the rest of their lives is incomplete or weakened. The relationship between parents and young children must include discipline. It must clearly not be one of equal status or the relationship will fail to yield mature, responsible adult children.

Children need clear structure and boundaries to be at peace with themselves. Otherwise, they function in a chaotic vacuum with no clarity or direction. The structure and boundaries that are enforced by discipline become a solid shelter from which they can observe and learn about the world around them.

Active Experimentation/Application

On my return to the family, I enforced discipline and respect for adults and their position. The immediate result was a great deal of friction and confrontation. Gradually, though, the relationship between Joy and me developed. When the physical and emotional boundaries were enforced, she became secure and comfortable within those boundaries. She could function as a two-year-old instead of being forced to function as a tiny adult. She then began to blossom and develop in ways that she had not been able to before.

I applied these same concepts in other areas of my life. I now assess at what level a person is functioning prior to deciding what might make an appropriate intervention. For instance, at work I don't expect too much from an employee learning something new. I make sure they're secure in a new task prior to giving them increased autonomy in it.

Reevaluating Boundaries

Just when a family seems to find a balance point for their collective "boat," some new changes force their reevaluation. Joy's dad relates this very adjustment in the following story.

Concrete Experience
All of the above sounds very wonderful, and it was. The appropriate maturity and behavior were very gratifying and made life much more peaceful. After a time, though, Joy began pushing her boundaries. There was increasing rebellion, argument, and disobedience in certain areas. Increased discipline seemed to have no effect, except in the very short-term.

Reflective Observation
In observing the change in behavior, and noting that increased discipline produced no prolonged change in behavior, I realized that she was outgrowing the boundaries placed around her.

Abstract Concepts
The first concept is that rebellion and argument may be symptomatic and not problematic. When the child outgrows the boundaries there will be chafing and discomfort for all involved. (Writing those words provided me with some insight that I need

now that she is seventeen and I am having some of the same problems again; maybe it is time to review boundaries. The learning never stops.)

Communication also changes with maturity, as the common basis of experience and understanding increases. With each passing year the parent is better able to relate to the child the reasons for certain requirements and standards. The discipline is replaced with understanding and, hopefully, willing compliance as the reasons become clear in the child's mind. The forms of discipline must also change with the maturity of the child. Whereas a very young child will not understand any form of discipline without *immediate* consequences for unacceptable behavior, an older child begins to understand that consequences for her actions may have long-term effects. Therefore harsh words or spankings may give way to restrictions or deprivations in some circumstances.

Active Experimentation/Application

As a result of our following these concepts, Joy's boundaries were changed and expanded. How we viewed and treated her reflected that she was maturing, not to mention that we were maturing and learning also. Our forms of discipline changed to reflect the ways that we were able to communicate. Her responsibilities were increased, and the standards for her work were raised. In short, I was learning to adjust to her maturing. Order and discipline were once again temporarily restored.

At work I have applied these same concepts. As a new employee grows in his understanding of the job, I am able to allow greater freedom. I can move from the "telling" mode of management to the "delegation" mode.

Moving to Self-Discipline

Joy's dad may never have heard of Jean Piaget but he has discovered that children of different ages have varying levels of cognitive development.

At some point, the child can both remember and internalize past behavior and its consequences. Joy was then able to enjoy different disciplining. As she grew, we grew as parents and our disciplining tool kit enlarged.

Concrete Experience
When she was subjected to consistent discipline for the first time at age two, there was a period of great friction. Gradually her attitudes and behavior improved as a result of that discipline. However, her behavior did not seem to make any noticeable improvement when she was with other people without Sue or me present.

Reflective Observation
It was obvious that Joy's behavioral changes were accommodations to the parental threat of discipline. The babysitter or others did not represent to her that same threat. Maintaining good behavior as a normal part of her life had not been imparted and she was not mature enough to make the association on her own.

Abstract Concepts
Self-discipline is a trait that requires maturity. Most parental training is directed toward behavior that will have widespread application in the child's life. However, the child must have sufficient understanding and maturity to perceive how that training is pertinent in applications other than the immediate situation. The parents' level of expectation and training with the child must be appropriate to the child's maturity. Children must learn self-discipline because they will spend most of their lives without any external disciplinarian present. Initially, the training of self-discipline with a small child often takes the form of threatening punishment for unsatisfactory behavior. As the child matures, she begins to grasp concepts about how behavior and events in the past affect the present situation. This is the foundation of self-discipline.

Active Experimentation/Application

I began using discipline after-the-fact, as in the case of Joy's poor behavior when we had left her with a babysitter. At first that discipline seemed to have no effect. She was not mature enough to relate the behavior to the discipline and was not aware of why she was being punished. Therefore, for a time, I did not punish her actions unless it was immediately after the deed.

At about age three, Joy seemed to have developed a sense of time; she could relate events in the past in a sensible way. When that occurred, I began to punish misbehavior that had taken place in the recent past. This time the results were apparent, as behavior patterns in our absence improved. She made comments such as "I was spanked after you (referring to a babysitter) were here last time because I was naughty." That ability to remember the behavior and relate it to discipline was the beginning of self-discipline. Improving her behavior in order to receive praise and avoid punishment was the beginning of learning to set goals.

Joy's dad discovers some important behavioral principles of psychology. Positive rewards reinforce more strongly than either punishment or negative reinforcement.

Creating Positive Incentives

Sometimes in the scramble of parents to adjust their techniques to their children's ever-changing needs, the spirit of love in discipline gets lost. I was able to recoup this spirit through positive incentives.

Concrete Experience

When she was approaching age two, Joy wanted lace underwear. She was told that the lace underwear was contingent upon toilet training; when she became dependable in that regard I would buy her the underwear. Soon the toilet training was accomplished.

Reflective Observation

Toilet training had become a source of frustration for us. We had come to the place where our positive training was not working. Discipline was consistently enforced with only minimal results. However, when the third concept, incentive, was added, the results were quickly forthcoming. Her attitude toward toilet training became much more positive and self-directed.

Abstract Concepts

Having a goal provided great impetus toward the desired behavior. Once a meaningful goal is established, it will frequently accomplish more, in less time, than punishment. Self-discipline is applied more readily and consistently toward the attainment of a worthwhile goal than toward the avoidance of punishment. Training provides the raw material for new behavior. Discipline defines the acceptable boundaries for behavior, but goals and incentives are frequently the catalyst that actually produces the change in behavior.

Active Experimentation/Application

We began to employ goals and incentives in training and discipline situations. Almost always the response was more positive and lasting when a goal was involved. When Joy was younger, the goals were short-term. As she matured, goals became more complex and long-term, but the principles remained the same. This was a major lesson for me as a parent. It taught me the value of positive dealings with children.

As children develop maturity and understanding, the reasons for self-discipline can be communicated more clearly and become interrelated with goals. In training and disciplining a child, the parent will get results that will almost always be quicker and longer lasting if the long-range benefits of the desired action can be communicated in a context that has meaningful appeal to the individual child. I discovered that positive goals that are within the realm of my daughter's understanding and that she could attain are a greater inducement to self-discipline and to her being open to training than is punishment.

Evolving an effective style:
"book-read" parent finds balance

Another parent describes her journey into discipline as a "book-read" adoptive parent who evolved from a permissive parent to an authoritarian parent, only to find her balance point through a method called "natural consequences." This parent's style revolves around Kolb's model at deeper levels until an effective long-term parenting style is discovered. In terms of executing Kolb's model, this student demonstrates exceptionally well the final section of the model, Active Experimentation/ Application.

Permissiveness

Becoming a new parent was one of the most thrilling events in my life. For years I had thought about what kind of parent I wanted to be. I had the highest expectations of myself. I knew I would be the perfect parent, always setting good examples and taking time and interest in all my child did. I also had formed very strong views on how I would discipline my child. This section will discuss the three different methods of discipline I tried. I started as a permissive parent, tried being an authoritarian, and ended up using a method of natural consequences to achieve the results I desired.

Concrete Experience

While my husband and I were waiting for the placement of a child from Catholic Social Services, I had a lot of time to study different ways in which to raise my child. My goal was to raise a child to become confident, competent, and independent, a fully functioning human being. After some prior study, I decided the only form of discipline to use was a very liberal approach. I was going to allow my child to develop freely and, if discipline was needed, I would talk things out with the child. I would be a friend first, then a mother. This was the form of discipline I decided would attain the best results. From the very start I continually talked to my child and explained everything. This system seemed to be working very well until my son started to become independent. When he started to explore the world around him, he no longer listened to me. As he grew and developed, it seemed as if I could no longer get his attention. He just wanted to scream, run around, and do what he wanted. I realized that early childhood was very difficult for both parent and child, so I tried to ignore his temper tantrums. I would try to calm him down and explain why he should not kick or bite. It seemed that every time I wanted him to behave, he would act up.

Because of my son's behavior toward other children, it was difficult for him to have friends. Many times I would call a friend on the phone and mention I wanted to stop by. I started noticing that my friends were making excuses in order not to have me visit. At first I thought I had done something offensive to cause my friends to act that way.

One day a friend of mine came in from California and stopped by to see me. We were both enjoying each other's company. Then the children began to fight. It seemed as if my son was always in the middle of the turmoil. He didn't want to share his toys. He was always ordering the other children around, and he always had to play what he wanted. From time to time I would stop my son and try to reason with him, but there was no way he was going to give in. After a while, my girlfriend made a remark that things hadn't changed since she had left; my son still did as he pleased. She asked if I anticipated having major problems with him when he entered young adulthood. At first, I was very shocked by her words. How dare she say something about my child's behavior. After all, I had read many of the psychology books and had decided this was the form of discipline a child needed to develop and grow.

Reflective Observations

As I write this paper, I remember how I reviewed all forms of discipline very carefully before I chose the one I felt worked the best for both parent and child in forming a strong relationship. I knew parents who were very strict with their children. Their children weren't able to make a sound. They were "to be seen and not heard." I had always felt this kind of discipline had an adverse effect on the child's personality.

Yet I was also very unhappy and troubled about my son's behavior. I kept wondering if I should reevaluate and change my method of disciplining. His behavior by our social norms was unacceptable. I had tried to just ignore it. I just kept reinforcing that a child has the right to grow up happy, and a happy child must be able to express himself freely. I remember many embarrassing situations where my son would talk back to me or just plain refuse to listen. At these times I would always question if I was handling his discipline in the correct manner.

When my friends would make remarks about other children's behavior or a child they knew who ruled his parents, I often wondered if they were referring to me. There were times when I was alone that I would just sit and wonder if I was making a mistake. Using a permissive approach was causing the loss of friends, not only for me but for my child. I was also experiencing very embarrassing situations, such as my son running away from me while I was talking to him. He lacked respect not only for me but for any person in authority. His teacher would call with the same complaints that my friends had: "Your son won't listen, he wants to do as he pleases, and he disrupts the class."

Abstract Concepts

Before becoming a parent, I had many discussions about my child and his life. Being young and never having had any experiences in child rearing, I referred to the so-called experts on the subject. I read a variety of books to learn techniques of parenting. I started to notice a pattern in the books. The books all seemed to concur that children shouldn't be spanked. This would only teach the children to strike out at someone when they got angry. The books also noted that children needed independence. Children needed to develop their own way. If a parent was demanding and excessive in discipline, the children wouldn't be able to learn independence.

After reading this material I wanted to give my son total freedom to learn and to handle new situations. I wanted him to become his own person without the confines of societal pressure. When I disapproved of his behavior, I accepted the behavior as an expression of himself.

The ideals of permissive parenting were my exact goals for child rearing. My child was going to be independent and confident. He would learn and develop without restrictions and become his own individual. However, the results that were achieved through permissive parenting were not what I had hoped. Instead he became unruly and out of control. Permissive parenting doesn't mean without discipline. I learned that a child needed direction to obtain these goals of independence and confidence.

Active Experimentation/Application

When I decided to become a permissive parent, I also became a permissive manager at work. I decided that my employees should handle their jobs independently and without my supervision. If a child would develop and learn more easily without control, adults under my management would perform their jobs more capably if given the freedom to do so.

I soon learned that as I lost control of my son, I also lost control of those I managed. Things which I felt were important to the company were not necessarily important to the people under me. Tasks were not completed on time and my department was not running efficiently. Since I was responsible to upper management, I needed to make a change at work as well as at home.

Authoritarian

Learning through our mistakes can be risky and hurtful as well as inefficient. Out of desperation I shifted to yet another style, reacting against what had not worked well.

Concrete Experience

I finally realized my approach to discipline was wrong for my son. The question now was whether I could turn the situation around. I decided to start over with a new technique. The permissive approach to discipline was not giving me the results I desired. Instead of researching a viable alternative, I began to discipline with the opposite approach. I became very strict and domineering. I started to watch my son like a hawk from the time he got up in the morning until the time he went to bed at night. I started by setting down rules which I wanted him to follow. Of course, after having total freedom, my son felt the rules were unfair and he was determined not to follow them.

Changing from a permissive parent to a disciplinarian was going to be a challenge. It was also going to take determination on my part. I knew I was going to have to follow through and check on him until his behavior was under control. After the list of rules was discussed so there was an understanding, I also discussed chores, time schedules, and behavior change. I set myself guidelines to apply a firm hand to turn around a serious problem. I had high hopes that my son's behavior problems would soon turn around, but the first week proved I wouldn't be that lucky.

Everything turned into a power struggle. I found myself having to discipline him more strongly and strictly. Everything was a continual battle. Enforcing even the smallest rule, like going to bed on time, became a major fight. The embarrassing situations when people would come over did not improve. It was as if he took that opportunity to challenge my newfound authority.

He also started to rebel at school by not completing his class work. He had always been a disturbance in class, but to make things worse he started fighting at school, his grades started to drop, and he wasn't doing any homework. He never did book reports, and he never did his assignments sheets; therefore, nothing was getting accomplished. I was spending more time at his school than ever.

17

I decided I needed to be even tougher. I started sitting with him at home while he did his homework. I practically walked him through it, night after night and subject after subject. I also arranged daily communication with the school. Thus I was always policing my son's behavior. By using an authoritarian form of discipline, I was only causing myself more work.

My behavior in dealing with my son changed, but I had no success in changing his behavior. Even if I had more control in a given situation, his habits and behavior returned and intensified when he was out of my control.

Reflective Observations

Changing the way in which a parent disciplines her child is very difficult. It not only has its effect on the child but also on the parent. As a parent who saw her mistake, it was initially very difficult to admit I had chosen the wrong form of discipline. I was forced into a complete turn around, always policing his actions. This drastic change was brought about in the hopes that it would help my son become a productive member of society.

Although this strict method of discipline had some good effects on both of us, the major problem with this form of discipline was that I was controlling my son's behavior. I had to check constantly on his work. I had to drive him to school and go inside and check with his teachers on a daily basis. I had to pick him up from school. Before we left, I had to check to see if he had all his work and if there were any problems during the day. This caused me to be very nervous. Due to my own mistake, I felt trapped by my son's behavior problems.

Abstract Concepts

As I had started to blame myself for all my son's troubles and failures, I looked around for an alternate discipline method. The method I turned to was a form of "Tough Love." I had seen a talk show where parents were interviewed about their children's discipline problems. They talked about having the same kind of problems I was having and how their method worked. So I started taking some notes as they spoke. I realized I would have to "start from scratch" and reteach my son a new form of behavior, but I would have to become tough. That night I made up my mind this is what my son needed, tough love.

Tough love or total authority is a method parents use on their children when they feel they have lost control of their children's lives as well as their own. Using this method, a parent has to set strict rules and follow through on them. The parent isn't to take any back talk from the child. The parent takes control of the child's life and after the parent feels the child can control himself, the parent can return some of the control. This method takes a long time and a lot of work by both the parent and child, and it requires parents to be on top of all situations. Because the child has already developed behavior problems, this method requires all the love, understanding, and the energy a parent has.

Of course, I was using my own interpretation of the method, and because of my own lack of experience and knowledge I found follow-through difficult. I know my son thought I had become the most unbearable person to live with because I started to enforce the rules, rules I felt would help him become a more productive human being.

Active Experimentation/Application

I sat my son down and explained the new method. Then I started to get tough. New rules were laid down and I started to enforce them. I started to take control of all situations. When I said "no," I meant it. His room had to be clean before he could go out. His homework had to be completed and done correctly before he could go out. If all the rules at home weren't followed, he was punished, and I saw that the punishment was fulfilled. When I told him he had to be home at a certain time and he was late, he was punished. He was accountable for all his actions and I was there to watch his every move. Every day there was more pressure being applied to my son's behavior, and I was becoming totally consumed by his life. The form of discipline I was using, the authoritarian method, was only working while I was on top of every situation. I started to feel as if I was living two lives, my son's and my own.

19

I had some doubts from the beginning, but I was desperate. I even tried this method with employees at work. If I had an employee who would not produce, I would become the police officer, always watching and suspecting every move. It always seemed that while I was Big Sister to the employees, things went well. The first time I started to back off, the employees reverted to their old habits. I began to see that being a police officer brought results from my employees and acceptable behavior in my son, but only when I as the authority figure was present. As long as I was in control of the situation, I received the results I expected. As soon as I distanced myself from the behavior, the behavior would return. No one was learning from this form of discipline. External authority only makes people behave while authority is present. It doesn't teach appropriate or productive behavior.

Natural Consequences

Desperately seeking an answer to an energy-draining situation, I sought professional help and finally discovered an answer for my son and me.

Concrete Experience

At this point I needed to turn to some other form of discipline, and I contacted a psychologist for new ideas and direction. My goal was still to teach my son self-confidence and self-control. I wanted a happy, well-adjusted child who exhibited acceptable behavior. The psychologist informed me that changing from one form of discipline to another was quite confusing to a child. She suggested I move very slowly in the transformation to another form of discipline. I met with the psychologist and discussed the methods I used as well as the problems I was encountering. Her answer was simply to choose a method down the middle of the road, something with which I was comfortable and with which I could stay. She told me what form of discipline she used with her children. She herself had read many of the same books on child rearing that I had. She agreed with some of them, although not with others. Because each child is so different, sometimes just an idea or part of an idea from a book can be successfully incorporated into a child's discipline.

What a parent needs is a form of discipline with which a child can grow. The doctor and I both agreed that a child needs to be responsible for his behavior. He must make his own decisions with a parent guiding him. She suggested a system she used; she called it "natural consequences." This system was devised so the child could learn and grow from his own mistakes. It would also take the pressure off me because I would no longer have to stand over my son every minute.

With the natural consequences system the child knows what is expected of him and also is told what will happen if he doesn't follow through. He then makes his own decisions on how to handle the situation. He makes his choice knowing all the facts. This sounded like a perfect way to restructure my son's behavior.

. Over the next few days I sat down with my son and we discussed obligations he had to himself as well as to others. I told him from now on he was going to be responsible for his work getting done in school, for his behavior with friends, and for chores being done. I explained that he was going to take control of his own actions and if he didn't follow through on his responsibilities, he would be the one who would suffer the consequences. I explained I no longer was going to run interference for him in any "way, shape or form."

Starting the next morning my son was given some tasks I wanted completed. I gave him a time limit. I told him how and what was expected of him. I also let him know what the consequences would be if he didn't complete these tasks. I also went to his school and informed them that from now on if he misbehaved and didn't do his assigned work he would be accountable for his actions. All the teachers I talked to agreed that they would deal with him in the same fashion. My new form of discipline and behavior modification was in action.

Reflective Observations

When I first learned of natural consequences, I started thinking back about aspects of all the books I had read and how

21

nothing worked in the past. I felt I had tried it both ways, being permissive and being authoritarian. Neither method had the desired effect.

Although my son had a difficult time handling his new freedom, he eventually realized that he had the freedom to decide for himself in all areas of his life. He started to accept and grow with this method. He started to accept responsibility on his own. He started doing his classwork in school. He knew if he didn't, he would have to stay out of gym. He started on his own to take control of his life. This system of discipline took time but accomplished the results I wanted and remains in effect today.

When my son's behavior began changing in a positive way, I started to change. I started to become more relaxed in my dealing with him. Now, for the first time in years, if a neighbor knocks on the door I am not concerned that she is there to complain about something my son has done. I started to feel more comfortable and confident in our relationship.

After some time, when my son started to behave in a much better manner, I started to feel proud of him. He still has some problems dealing with his temper, but, compared with his behavior before he is very much improved. By using natural consequences as my way of disciplining my child, I've become more aware of my child's needs. He needed guidance, not punishment. He needed independence, not my control. I now know a parent must walk a tightrope in handling discipline problems. Each parent must find the method that works with his or her own child.

Abstract Concepts

Because I was having problems handling my son's behavior, I went to seek help from an outside source. This was the best decision I made, not only for my son but for myself. By working closely with the psychologist, I could incorporate a form of discipline which was effective for my son. The psychologist, as a parent herself, seemed to understand how important child rearing is. She introduced me to a book on stepparenting. This book talked about teaching a child natural consequences as a method of discipline. The book explained that a child must understand what the rules are and what will happen to him if he breaks the rules. My son soon realized he would be responsible for his own actions. I learned that a child should take responsibility for his own actions. One day he will be an adult and be responsible for his life.

In a book I read on stepparenting, I found detailed instructions. It laid out natural consequences as a form of discipline. The child is taught to be responsible for his own behavior through both firmness and example. As an example, if it is the child's responsibility to take a lunch to school and the lunch is forgotten, the child goes hungry. The parent does not rush to school with the lunch.

As a form of discipline, natural consequences develops as the child develops. As the child's responsibilities increase, the consequences increase. If responsibility is taught early in his life, later on, when more important subjects such as sex are discussed, the responsibility is accepted and understood.

Active Experimentation/Application

Not only did this method work with my son but I applied the same method to my work situation. I now tell employees what is expected of them, how much time they have to complete a job, and what will happen to them if the job isn't completed. I find employees work better under these conditions. It gives the employees some control over the situation because it gives them some choices. My employees are familiar with the consequences of not completing a job in the time frame given. If the consequence is the loss of job, the employees themselves are responsible for the outcome.

I learned from my experience that a person must not assume that something will work merely because it is written in a book by some "expert." I read many books about discipline, but it took experience to make a technique work. I also learned that being either too permissive or too strict wasn't effective for my child. A parent must have a system which can be continued as a child grows. The method of natural consequences was the answer for me.

Bridging different styles:
a stepparent's guide

The final adult to relate her learning through experience is a stepmother. She gives us an excellent example of the tension between mates which differing approaches to discipline can cause.

Approaching A Problem

I can say that my stepson is hardly ever a disciplinary problem. However, I would not be completely truthful if I said we never had any problems. He is now twelve years old, and over the years certain problems have come up that have needed assistance.

We meet these problems in quite different ways, although my husband and I never really talked about the discipline of Scott. My husband is one that will talk a problem to death, while I am more inclined to discuss it and then take some kind of action if the problem continues. Tom was always very good about discussing problems with Scott and had a lot more patience with him than I did.

Concrete Experience

One incident that comes to mind happened in a local restaurant. Scott has a tendency to get sick when he eats too much junk food. We had gone out for tacos and we ordered Cokes for everyone. Scott proceeded to drink his down. I ordered him another one and told him that that was the last one he was getting and to drink it sparingly. A few minutes later he got up from the table and disappeared. When he came back, he had another Coke in his hand. I asked him where he got it and he said at the front counter. I asked him what I had said about more Coke and he stated to me that I had told him that he could not have another. I could not believe that he disobeyed me so blatantly. I told him that when we got home he was to give me the joysticks to his computer and he was not to use it for the rest of the week. At this point my husband became very aggravated at me in front of Scott. He said he thought that I was rather hard on him, and he thought I should rethink my position. I told him we would discuss it later at home.

When we got home, I was angry at my husband and told him so. I told him that no matter how he felt about the punishment I gave Scott, I expected him to support me. If he did not agree with me, we could discuss it in private later. I remember this incident causing a lot of hard feelings between the two of us.

We both shared in the punishment of Scott when it was necessary. This could range from sending him to his room to taking his computer away. We found over the years that the computer was the most effective punishment. Scott loved his computer and spent hours playing with it.

We were also very fortunate that we keep a fairly good relationship with Scott's mother. Several times she called us to tell us about a problem she was having with Scott and wondered if Tom would talk to him. This seemed to be very effective, in that Scott knew that his mother and father were in contact with each other and supported the discipline the other one imposed. I feel that this gave Scott the message that everyone was united in his discipline.

Reflective Observations

In reflecting on how we dealt with Scott, I feel that our methods were very effective. We had very few problems with Scott. When something did come up, we tried to talk about it with him and explain to him what was wrong with his behavior. That usually worked.

When something more serious came up, it took several incidents for Tom and me to agree on how to deal with it. I feel that constant communication between Tom and me helped. Once he knew my feelings—that I expected him to support me on my decisions—things seemed to smooth out.

I still feel that Tom is sometimes too easy on Scott. Scott has since moved to Florida. We only get him every summer for ten weeks and every other Christmas. When we do have Scott, Tom lets him get away with things that I'm sure he wouldn't if Scott were with us all the time. I don't think this is to Scott's advantage, but again, as the stepparent, I know when to keep quiet.

Abstract Concepts

In Emily and John Visher's book *Stepfamilies: A Guide to Working With Stepparents & Stepchildren,*[4] they write about the problem of discipline in stepfamilies. They suggested that stepchildren are more receptive to discipline by the stepparent after they have developed a good relationship. There are often problems when the stepparent comes into the picture and starts to institute punishment before any type of a relationship is developed. I think that this is an excellent point. I have found that since the closeness between the two of us was established he has not resented being punished by me. He never gives me any problems when I discipline him and always accepts it as if his father had punished him.

June and William Noble also point out that it is important to be fair in disciplining the children and in setting up an expected pattern and sticking to it.[5] Consistency is important. If children know what to expect, it is easier to enforce rules. This is more difficult in families with parents in different homes; children with several sets of parents need special attention to communication for consistency's sake.

Active Experimentation/Application

Over time my husband and I have refined our disciplining approach with Scott. We have learned to support one another and be consistent with discipline. Tom and I continue to keep lines of communication open with each other and with Scott. This provides us with a united front.

These same principles can apply in the workplace. As I work with other employees, keeping lines of communication open is important in building a team and maintaining relationships. With employees I know it is important to build a solid and trusted relationship before I can attempt to discipline.

It seems as if these parents have learned what Baumrind discovered over twenty years ago. Parental styles reflect four dimensions:

    —parental control
    —parent-child communication
    —maturity, demands for achievement
    —nurturance

The authoritative parent scores high on all four dimensions. W. Becker, et al., discovered that the children of authoritative parents showed "the most desirable personal qualities, as judged by the standards of our society: they are the most self-reliant and self-controlled, yet also the friendliest and highest achieving."[6]

Although family contexts differ, the need for discipline remains constant. Finding the proper keel is an authentic need for each family. Some learning from experience on this topic is summarized.

Adult Learning Through Life Experience

or

THINGS I WISH SOMEBODY HAD TOLD ME

—Raising a lovable child without some tough decisions and tearful moments cannot be done. Things are not always peachy in rearing children to be responsible persons.

—It is best to start early with caring discipline because it only gets tougher as children get older.

—Children grow into secure adults if parents' rules are explicit and clear when children are younger; consequences need to be predictable.

—Patience and noise are to be expected in rearing children.

—Parenting is dynamic; its strategies need review with each new stage of a child's ever-changing development.

Chapter Two

From lemons to lemonade:
Transforming problems into possibilities

Natalie Gianetti

Growing up in the 1940s and 1950s in a small, Upper Peninsula town in Michigan gave me a limited picture of the family and parenting. After all, didn't all fathers go to work and all mothers stay home with the children planning outings and entertainment? Marriage, five children, a divorce, working as a single parent and remarriage all contributed to my altered view of the family and parenting.

According to Christopher Lasch, the contemporary American family is made up of parents who work away from the home and children who spend early years in child care centers or with babysitters and are later educated in schools.[1] Blended families have become another configuration of the American family.

As I work with the adult students who are writing life learning papers, I am aware that they exemplify contemporary American families. Many of these students are working parents who are married, single, or in a blended family situation. They have been faced with many problem situations as they attempt to parent and/ or stepparent in today's society. Each has faced his or her situations and moved for acceptable, positive solutions in varied and unique ways.

They have taken lemons and made lemonade.

Providing secure care:
a single working mom's dilemma

A single working mother faces many dilemmas when parenting. This mother must handle babysitting needs and the sickness of her children as she works to meet financial needs. She feels her situation helped to instill responsibility, independence and self-sufficiency in her children. In the process she learned from them.

Child Care Choices

For most of my years as a single parent, it was a financial necessity that I work. Working as a single parent proved to be very challenging with many different aspects to be considered, including baby-sitters, day care and ill children.

Concrete Experience

In the beginning of my working outside the home, neither child was in school. It was necessary to hire a babysitter. Hiring a competent sitter who was liked by the children and me was time-consuming and frustrating, but we finally found one who took children into her home. This meant waking the children early to take them to the sitter's and then going to work myself. To make the situation easier for the children, I would let them choose two different toys to take with them each day. I also set aside the first hour after we returned home to talk with them about their day.

When the older child began school, the younger child went to day care and a sitter came into the home after school until I returned home. Day care worked out so well that I chose to use the day care for both children, with the older child attending the day care summer program. We used day care for nearly three years. After this time, the children were both in school, and I again decided to have a sitter come in after school. A few years later the children went to a neighbor's after school. This neighbor was a

30

friend who had children close in age to mine, so it was a near-perfect situation. As the children grew older and more responsible, they were allowed to remain home alone for the three hours after school. They were given specific instructions and were allowed a prepared snack; I would call to check on them.

Another area that working parents have to deal with is the ill child. My children were not often ill, but when they were it was usually at different times. They went through the usual colds, flu, chicken pox and stomach aches. When my children were ill, they wanted and needed me, so I stayed home with them and lost time at work.

When ill, my children were usually cranky and demanding. Because I had to stay home with the ill child, I spent more time with him doing what he wanted. Since I had two children, the one who was not ill became somewhat jealous, so I had to include that child in the routine. The ill child's room became the center of activity. Everything took place there. When the ill child became better, I would move our center of activity elsewhere, usually to the kitchen. When the child was well enough to return to normal activity, there was a feeling of having finished an adventure.

Reflective Observations

Life as a working single parent was tiring, busy, complicated and sometimes frightening. Trying to insure that the children did not feel neglected was one of my major concerns. I spent a large part of my free time with them to help them avoid experiencing those feelings.

It was necessary that I work, and I had to try to help the children realize this. The children were young, but they came to realize that my working was part of our lives. My working helped the children develop a sense of responsibility. They had their chores to perform and I had mine. We all had adventures to share which helped to enrich our lives. My being a working single parent helped the children realize that working to earn a living was what was acceptable and expected in our society. My working also helped them see females as people who could do other things besides mothering and homemaking.

31

As the children grew older, they were able to give more help around our home. They were also old enough to realize exactly how much I had been doing during the past years. They were now ten and thirteen years of age. Now I decided that they needed to be aware of our family's financial situation. So one of our "round table" discussions took place. This had a positive effect on them. They now felt a real part of the family. They told me that they were afraid when they did not know what was going on.

As I now look back on how I dealt with working and rearing the children, I realize that we made the best of a situation. The children are now seventeen and twenty years old, and they both are wage earners. They both know that they will have to work to be able to succeed, and they accept this.

Abstract Concepts

Being a working single parent while the children were young was not what I had planned. However, circumstances demanded that particular choice. During those years the children grew into responsible, independent and self-sufficient people. They learned from our situation and from me. I also learned from them and grew into a more mature adult.

There were problems, but never to the degree that we could not work them out. Those years of our lives saw a rapid amount of growth for all of us and resulted in my developing some ideas about the single parent who has to work:

—Children, even young ones, can understand and accept certain situations if the situation is presented in the proper manner.

—Children respond in a positive manner when given age-appropriate responsibilities.

—By seeing their parents performing in roles that have traditionally been specifically male or female, children learn that they also have choices and are not limited within gender-specific roles.

—Children should be kept aware of the family's financial situation. However, this does not mean that they should be made to feel responsible for or burdened with the family finances and obligations.

Active Experimentation/Application

The ideas I have developed are from my own experiences as a working single parent. Initially, these ideas were my ways of handling a difficult situation. Others have asked how I managed to work and take care of the children; I've asked myself that same question. My answer usually involves passing on some of my ideas to them. Most single parents work out of necessity. They have no real choice.

When I realized that I would have to work and it would probably be for several years, I began to think of the needs of the children. Since my son was the older child, I could develop some of my ideas through him and further develop them with my daughter. I made mental plans for them when they were young and then began to implement those plans. Every single working parent that I have spoken with has done similar things. The ideal has been that every home had a mother and a father. The father worked while the mother stayed home with the children. This was not my situation, and the difference had to be addressed. These ideas worked with my children and can possibly work for others.

Building quality time:
a stepmom's experience

Stepparenting involves an added dimension to problem situations in a family. When one has the child only part of the time, it becomes important to make the best use of that time yet provide love and discipline in the process. The following woman describes ways in which she addresses quality time parenting of a stepson she has for a limited time each month.

Quality Time Versus Quantity Time

According to J. Dugger, "Kids aren't looking for quality or quantity time, they're just looking for time with you. Sometimes that involves interaction, but other times it's just being in the same room with you."[2]

Quality time is a phrase of the eighties that has fallen from favor in the nineties. What I mean by "quality time," however, is "making the most of the time allotted to me."

Concrete Experience

Sunday mornings are my favorite time with my stepson, Doug. He and I are both early risers. My husband doesn't usually make an appearance before ten. Doug usually wakes me up before seven. Together we make blueberry muffins. It has become a ritual in our house. We eat muffins while we sit closely together on the couch, usually working in a workbook, doing activities in the *Highlights* magazine, reading the comics from the Sunday paper, or reading one of Doug's many Dr. Seuss books. No television, just us. This is quality time. This sets the tone for the rest of the day.

Reflective Observations

Children need to have time with their parents—one-on-one time, with no distractions, not being entertained but doing the entertaining. I have learned from Doug's mother that he watches television from the time he gets home from school until the time he goes to bed. On Saturday, he watches cartoons all morning. He knows what time it is by what he is watching on television. When he is at our house, he never asks to turn on the television, nor does he request even his favorite shows. The television has become a form of babysitting at his home. We do not have the luxury of day-to-day time with Doug, so every time he visits I try to make some part of his visit quality time.

I can tell how much more calm and relaxed Doug is when he is doing something with us. A good example was last year when he and I carved a pumpkin. We worked out a plan, and then we carried it through. He was so happy. Those are the days when he doesn't want to let go when he hugs me good-bye.

It is very hard for me to set standards and live by them. I think about Doug a lot. Are we doing all we can for him? Can we do things better? Differently? I wonder what it is like for him to be shuffled back and forth so much. Our life-styles are so different from his mother's. Our standards are different. What will he be like when he gets a little older? I hope he has happy memories of his childhood. For all the changes he has had to cope with in his young life, he seems very well adjusted. He is well cared for and loved by both sets of parents.

Abstract Concepts

Quality time is time spent with one's child, with no outside interference. It is time where the parent and child can communicate with each other. The child's time is as important as the adult's time. Quality time means doing things together.

Children know when they have a parent's attention and they know when they do not. Children can sense when others are holding back or are distracted. They take this inattention as a lack of caring for them and the things that interest them.

Quality time is the time spent communicating with a child. It is a time when a parent can share with him, and he can share with the parent.

Active Experimentation/Application

My husband and I need quality time together, whether it be pillow talk, mealtime conversation, or a face-to-face discussion. We need uninterrupted time together. Our time is very special. It is during these times we catch up on each other's career; we share in each other's accomplishments; we offer encouragement. When we are in need, we supply each other with whatever is needed.

It is our time together and it is vital, yet that time seems so hard to find. Between work, school, homework, housework, and whatever else comes between us, we only have so much time together. We try to make it memorable. Quality time is memorable time.

Making good use of time:
a long distance relationship

In this next example of a challenging situation, a Michigan stepmother writes about facing parenting and the building of a relationship with a stepchild who has moved to Florida. The adjustments for her are more difficult as she sees her stepson for only ten weeks in the summer. She demonstrates ways of using quality time in parenting.

Time and Distance Factors

Children are not easy to raise in any family, but for stepparents it is doubly difficult. There are no set rules for stepparents, and most families that are faced with this situation simply try and "muddle" through it the best they can. This becomes even more difficult when parents do not have physical custody of the children and then must become part-time parents.

Concrete Experience

When I first met Scott, my husband Tom had him every other weekend and every other Christmas. Scott lived about six miles from us, and we often got him during the week for special occasions. For our weekend time, we planned family activities. This could be canoeing, swimming or just cooking out in the backyard. If we made plans of any kind, Scott was included in them.

Approximately three years ago, Scott, his mother and stepfather moved to Florida. This was a big loss to us. We went from having Scott every other weekend to having him every other Christmas and ten weeks during the summer. It was a very big adjustment for us all. I remember the last weekend we spent together before they moved. We talked about staying in touch; however, we knew that our relationship would never be the same.

37

Since Scott has moved, we talk to him weekly on the telephone. He calls us on Saturday night and we discuss his week. This includes everything from school to the latest games he's playing. We have also encouraged him to call us any time he wants. While this is not an ideal situation, we are trying to make the best of a bad situation.

When we do get him during the summer, his visits mean even more to us than before. We realize how precious these times are and how quickly they will be over. The principle of quality time instead of quantity time certainly applies in our situation. We have found how important it is to carefully plan our activities and family vacations to include the whole family. All of these build memories that Scott can take home with him. Many phone calls have been spent simply remembering some good times that we shared during the summer vacations. While he may be geographically distant, these memories seem to bring us closer to each other.

It may not seem like a telephone call once a week is a lot. However, I feel that these calls keep us fully involved in Scott's life. We discuss everything and anything and, even though we are apart, we know exactly what is going on in his life. We make sure that he is aware of what is happening at our home with the house and the cat.

We also keep Scott informed of what is new with all his grandparents, aunts, uncles and cousins. He likes to hear the stories about our weekends at grandma and grandpa's, even though he was not there. All of these things are crucial for our relationship with Scott.

Reflective Observations

In looking back at the relationship with Scott since he has moved, I feel that we have done the best we can to keep our relationship with him strong. I have found that the amount of time spent with the child is not nearly as important as the quality of time. I feel very strongly that parents can spend all day with their child and still not know what is going on in his life. While we do not have a lot of time to spend with Scott, the time that we do have is spent in meaningful activities. Reading him a bedtime story and then lying on the bed talking with him has produced some interesting conversations. I find that while Scott is only twelve years old, he has a lot of things going on inside of him. If I just take the time to talk with him, it comes out.

Abstract Concepts

In Anne W. Simon's *Stepchild in the Family*, she states that children need quality time spent with them.[3] She writes that, while many stepfamilies do not have physical custody of the children all the time, the time they do have needs to be spent sharing things in their lives. Getting the children on the weekend and dropping them off on Sunday night with no interaction can result in a breakdown in communication between family members.

I am very pleased with the relationship that has developed between Scott and me. However, it was not a relationship that came overnight. It had to be cultivated and worked at. We went from having Scott every other weekend to having him only ten weeks a year; this was a big adjustment. However, even though the amount of time has dropped dramatically, the relationship has not been severely affected. I feel that we are still very close. I realize that the distance alone makes it impossible to have the same kind of relationship we had with Scott when he was in town. However, I feel it is as strong.

Active Experimentation/Application

I think that the principle of quality versus quantity time can be applied to almost any relationship. Because my husband and I both have busy schedules, we do not always have a lot of time to spend together. However, when we do have time, we try to spend it talking or doing something together. I feel that this is important to any relationship.

I am also very much aware of how important it is to stay in touch with Scott. While the few minutes we spend on the phone each week may not seem like much, it is important for keeping the lines of communication open. Having been in Scott's life for over five years, I can sense when something is wrong with him. He will tell us over the phone there is nothing wrong, but troubles eventually come out, and he talks to us about them. I do not think I would pick up on those kinds of things if we did not spend those few minutes each week together on the phone.

Overcoming background baggage: a father's commitment

Our last example is from a man who discusses parenting from his own negative experiences as a child. Through these negative experiences, he has determined to be a positive model in his role as a parent. He clearly made lemonade from lemons! This is a consistent pattern throughout life learning papers on parenting; adult students describe either modeling their parents' style: respecting and admiring it, or they use their parents' style as a model for everything they do not want for their children.

The Responsibilities of Fatherhood

Being a father is an enormous responsibility that requires much more than one may idly conceive. From infancy to adulthood the child requires love, guidance, discipline and nurturing. The level of quality at which a father performs his role largely depends upon how much time and effort he commits. It also depends upon how the father perceives his role. If he values his role and his relationship with his child, he will unfold the knowledge and wisdom from the many experiences he has had. He will learn from his mistakes and take the many opportunities to understand the needs of his child and his fatherly responsibilities.

Concrete Experiences
My parents divorced when I was three. Although my father has been an inspiration to me and a great influence on my values and morals, I did not live with him. Therefore, I have had some awful experiences resulting from a childhood with an absent father.

My mother and stepfather fought with each other routinely. Sometimes my stepfather would hit my mother, and sometimes my mother would throw household items at my stepfather. Both of them were usually drinking quite heavily when the initial argument started.

The majority of memories I have of my stepfather are of him sitting around the house. I remember a short period one summer when he would take me to baseball practice. He did not stay to watch me but returned home. Usually I got a ride from one of the other parents that stayed to watch his child.

My stepfather rarely let me bring any of my friends into the house. The only friends I would personally consider inviting into our house were the ones that I knew really well. This was because I was ashamed of the appearance of the interior of our home. Additionally, my stepfather could be very rude to my friends. I remember him ordering us out to the backyard because we did not need to be in the house. I guess this would not be so significant except it was rare that we were in the house.

Neither my stepfather or my mother ever initiated my involvement in any extracurricular activities. I was rarely permitted to get involved. My friends were the only initiators. Getting involved is what my stepfather and mother never did. They rarely got involved in anything for my benefit.

I recall this as being the way it was around our house. The only thing my stepfather ever did was tell me what to do or what not to do. Never did he set a good example as a friend or parent. My mother could not do it all herself. She worked her best at supporting us. She also drank too much, which affected the quality of her parenting.

Reflective Observations

I wish that my childhood could have been better. I know that it was a really rotten way to be raised. I cried many times, as I felt sorry for myself and was jealous of almost any other child I knew. I hated my environment but was powerless to do anything about it.

I had already tried to improve my life by spending more time with my father during the summer. Although things at my dad's were not what I wished, the atmosphere was more consistent with what I envisioned a child's life ought to be like. My life there was better but still not right, because my stepmother had her own children, and my presence there felt like an intrusion. This made me eventually cut back on the duration of my visits.

Abstract Concepts

My childhood offered me a special understanding of the necessary elements for a well-rounded upbringing. Foremost, the lack of love from a father figure which I experienced stands out as the single most important element present during my childhood years. Secondly, the basic foundation of stability and respect was absent as well. These two elements formed an emptiness that was only partially filled through the distant presence of my real father.

When the psychological issues are analyzed in normal childhood development, there is personal and theoretical evidence to indicate that the love of a parent results in the child's mirrored ability to love. I had a difficult time offering love until I experienced the concept enough times through my own maturation. As Benjamin Spock so aptly stated:

> The greatest gift from parents is love, which they express in countless ways: a fond facial expression, spontaneous demonstrations of physical affection, pleasure in their children's accomplishments, comforting them when they are hurt or frightened, controlling them to keep them safe and to help them become responsible loving children. It is from this lovingness toward parents that children go on to form their positive relationships in life.[4]

Active Experimentation/Application

Because of the misfortunes of my childhood and the unique relationship with my stepfather, an everlasting awareness is embedded within my value structure as to what my two sons require for building strong characters. I also became aware of how the closeness of a tightly knit family would allow my sons to develop and mature without the psychological problems I felt I incurred.

An example of my parental awareness is my unwavering desire to praise my sons' accomplishments, to begin to build their self-esteem. Where there are little failures, I praise their attempts and urge their continued efforts. My children are still young. Therefore, "little" tasks are sometimes big obstacles for them to overcome. When they are challenged, it is usually harder for them to continue trying than to give up. Therefore, it is important to make their continued effort result in a bigger reward than if they give up without attempting the challenge.

Since failure can cause emotional depression, it is important to help a child realize that failure is a part of life and that failure can give insight to persistence. This concept is not one that can be explained to a young child, but it can be demonstrated. Demonstration comes from attempting something and purposely failing. Silly facial expressions and exaggerated demonstrations can be played out to show how failure can be viewed comically. It can also be demonstrated how failure can teach new insights for the next attempt. If we learn from our mistakes, they become merely temporary setbacks, informative sources of learning for the next attempt.

Experience is an excellent teacher. Absence of an experience can also be an excellent teacher. I hope that what I missed when I was growing up will make me a much better father. I will never forget what it was like to have missed the closeness of a tightly knit family and a tightly knit father-son relationship within a happy home.

Today, as a father to two boys, I have the control to develop and groom our relationship. I am very aware of their needs for closeness and respond with zeal to offer them myself in every way that is appropriate to the situation. In their minds there is no doubt that their "daddy" is a loving role model and that they can count on me to be there to share quality time with them.

Parenting offers many challenges. If we can move from lemons to lemonade through our parenting experiences, our learning and growth become positive and rewarding. The following concepts are an outgrowth of the student learning.

Adult Learning Through Life Experience
or
THINGS I WISH SOMEBODY HAD TOLD ME

—People aren't able to control or know every eventuality that life might bring.

—It is important to accept what has gone wrong, to try to take a negative and transform it into a challenge, something from which to grow.

—"Quality time" is memory-making; it may consist of such simple things as the quiet of everyday rhythms lived out together, as well as more special events.

—If problems are made explicit, children can adapt and retain good feeling despite their having to accept extra duties, great frugality or physical distance between them and the parent. Creative responses and alternatives are usually available.

—Sometimes a negative model is motivation for counter "modeling" to the good.

Chapter Three

Parenting traditions across cultures

Barbara Cherem

The traditions of family life in the United States are probably as diverse as those of any place in the world. A nation of immigrants, America has borrowed heavily from around the world. As Thomas Sowell so aptly describes in Ethnic America, some of the immigrants' traditions readily matched America's prevailing culture, whereas others were less able to accommodate.[1] Sowell provides an understanding of the history of such archetypes as the protective Polish mother and the Russian "babushka." He illustrates how adaptive certain traditions were to American niches. For example, Sowell explains how Russian Jews held traditions which had their mothers taking sewing work into their homes, thus aligning themselves with the garment industry. Women in other immigrant groups, such as the Irish, often became maids in others' homes. Some traditions from the "sending" culture carry into American families today.

The two stories in this chapter come from very different family traditions. The first story explains the matriarchy of this particular family derived from its African-American heritage. Polygamy is mentioned from the perspective of a Nigerian relative, as a practice with a history in a certain time and place.

The second family is more recently cross-cultural in that the woman mothered her two children in India while her spouse studied and worked in America. Later, the woman and her two children joined her spouse in America, where she continued her parenting of "two children to be hybrids of two cultures."

47

These two stories take the reader on unique family journeys. In today's shrinking world, so thoroughly connected via quick communication and transportation, cross-cultural family stories seem an appropriate inclusion in any volume on parenting.

Continuing a matriarchy:
an African-American experience

Establishing the Matriarchy

I don't remember Mr. Game. He died before I was born. Family discussions have left me with a strong impression of who he was. He was a much older man than my grandmother. For many years, he was the head of our traditional nuclear family.

Mr. Game and my grandmother had eight children. It was my grandmother's duty to care for the children and keep them out of Mr. Game's way.

He was an aloof, undemonstrative man. None of the children tell of warm intimate times shared with him: no "fishing with Dad" stories, no heart-to-heart talks, no long walks. That all of his natural children call him "Mr. Game" is testimony to his emotional distance from them.

Mr. Game was the absolute ruler of the family until he became ill and my grandmother took care of him. There was no role reversal during his lifetime.

Our family became a matriarchy after the death of Mr. Game, my grandfather. My grandmother was left with a family of young adults and teens. She not only influenced the lives of her teenage children still at home but also the lives of her married adult children away from home. Since her authority reached outside the nuclear family into the extended family, she was not just a single parent, but the matriarch.

I started learning my parenting style from my grandmother as I watched her intervene in the parenting of her grandchildren as babies and as teenagers. With the death in a family, the head of the family may change. This happened in my family and thus resulted in the emergence of a matriarch. I will discuss the emergence of the matriarch in the Curry family, parenting different age groups, and the changing of the matriarchy.

Concrete Experience

When my grandfather died, my grandmother became the single head of the household. Living in the home with her were four of her children and one grandchild. There were my Uncle Bill, a single young man; my aunts Ann and Martha; and my mother. They were all teenagers. My cousin Curtis, a toddler, lived in grandma's household too. Curtis' mother, Hannah, lived not far away with her husband and baby son, Billy. It was my grandmother's decision to keep Curtis until she was sure that his stepfather would treat him well.

There also were two other uncles. Sandy lived nearby with his wife. Samuel, the oldest boy, had moved far away and was not close to the family even before my grandfather's death. There may have been a serious disagreement between my grandfather and him.

A couple of years after my grandfather's death, I was born to my then unwed mother. In the interim, the older teenage girls had moved; one married, and the other went north to find a job.

My mother married when I was a toddler and moved north with her new husband. My Aunt Hannah divorced her husband and moved north to live with Ann and find a job.

My grandmother would not allow any of her three grandchildren to be taken north into such uncertainty. Hannah's two children, Curtis and Billy, and I remained with her.

After a year, Hannah asked Momma (I called my grandmother "Momma" because everyone else did) if she could have her sons with her in Washington, D.C. Momma traveled by bus to Washington, D.C. with the two boys and me. After she had looked around at Aunt Hannah and Aunt Ann's environment, apartments, and neighborhood, and ascertained how they were living, she left the boys. She and I went back to Arkansas.

We traveled a lot during my preschool years. We made long visits to each of her children: Bill, Hannah, Samuel, Ann and my mother, Ollie. When it was time for me to start school, she took me to my Aunt Hannah's house to be raised with my cousins, Curtis and Billy.

50

Reflective Observations

Even though the family was not under the same roof, they were all under the authority of the matriarch, my grandmother, Betty. When Hannah got married, it was with Momma's permission and with the understanding that she could move, but that Curtis, Hannah's toddler son, would stay.

Uncle Bill remained unmarried. He moved out of the family home for a short time, but he returned to help the family financially as the third generation grew. He contributed financially but was not the decision-maker.

All who left Momma's house left with permission, except Martha, who ran away to get married. Momma was not involved in the day-to-day decisions that were made, but she communicated with them all by letters, visiting, and later by telephone. Sometimes a special trip was made in troubled times to smooth things over. With relatively quick mass transportation within an affordable range and the availability of telephones, it was possible to control a family from any point, as it is possiblem to manage a large corporation from a distance.

According to the traditional definition of extended family, our family was not one. Yet looking closely at the family dynamics, it was indeed an extended family.

Abstract Concepts

Billingsley identifies twelve types of family structures (see Table 1) eight of which are headed by husband and wife.[2] There are three nuclear-type families, starting with husband and wife only. This is called the incipient nuclear family. The addition of children changes the classification to a simple nuclear family. A single-parent head of household family is classified as an attenuated nuclear family.

There are three classifications of extended families: simple, consisting of husband and wife, children and other relatives; incipient, consisting of husband and wife, no children or other relatives; and the attenuated extended family, which has a single head of household.

51

Augmented families consist of different combinations of the above with the addition of non-relatives. They are listed in Table 1 as the incipient augmented family, the incipient extended augmented family, the nuclear extended augmented family, the attenuated augmented family, and the attenuated extended augmented family.

Horton and Hunt describe the extended family as a joint or consanguine family.[3] The core of the consanguine family is a group of brothers and sisters surrounded by a fringe of husbands and wives. In this type of family, affection and responsibility are widely spread throughout the group of people. Children are the joint responsibility of the entire family. Such a family has many positive effects. The consanguine family protects the individual against misfortune. If a child's mother or father dies or is otherwise incapacitated, other family members move easily into their roles. There is little danger of loneliness or neglect. This was the Curry family type.

In this paper, three generations will be discussed. For clarification, "Momma" (the author's grandmother) belongs to the first generation, her children will be referred to the "second generation," and their children are the "third generation."

Active Experimentation/Application

Recently, my daughter got married. She is twenty-five years old and a college graduate, and she has been independent for several years. Her husband is Nigerian, thirty years old, and an engineering student.

I learned a few things about Femi before he became my son-in-law. He has lived away from home since he was eleven years old, attending a private boarding school, then school in Yugoslavia and in the United States. He is the third in a family of ten. His father is a businessman in his seventies. Femi is the product of an extended family.

His grandmothers were nearby and active in his life when he was growing up. The most astonishing thing for me is that he has two mothers! His father is married to two women. They all live under one roof, though they do have so-called apartments within the same building.

I was vastly interested in this cultural difference. Femi and I talked at great length about his childhood relationship with the two women. Having studied and experienced parenting, I knew of the strong effect the family has on the attitudes of the child.

He explained to me that polygamy was the way of the older generation, and that few of the younger people were selecting polygamy as a life style; moreover, some of them looked down on the practice.

Femi was not embarrassed by the lifestyle of his family. It was all he knew. He explained that the first few years of his life he didn't know who his biological mother was. His needs were met by either mother, with no differentiation between offspring. All of the siblings are brothers and sisters. I have never heard him use the terms "half brother" or "half sister."

I learned that the two-mother family of Nigeria is a variation of our own extended family, offering Femi the same positive effects in his culture of Nigeria. Femi had a working mother. He also had a mother who was at home when he came home from school. He had mothers and grandmothers who nurtured and took care of him when he was sick and taught him the values he would live by as an adult. It is reminiscent of the childrearing of the Israeli kibbutz.

By age eleven, he was fortified enough to be able to leave home to go to school. When he talks about his childhood, I see pleasure in his eyes and a faint smile on his lips. I feel certain that as a child Femi was seldom lonely and never felt unloved.

Changing the Family Structure

As our family matured and third-generation children reached adulthood, it became more and more common to have single-parent households within the extended family structure. There were many reasons for the growth of the single-parent family. It was a reflection of society due to divorce and the increase of children born out of wedlock. Sadly, death of the father was also a factor.

Concrete Experience

When I was twenty-five, I became part of a single-parent family. My husband was killed in an accident when we had two small children and I was expecting another. There was never any other option except to raise my children myself.

We were living in Minnesota at that time. I had in-laws there, but no blood relatives. I decided to move closer to my family. I chose to move to Detroit where Aunt Ann was living. She had the most stable home life. She was "down to earth," rational, and a less emotional thinker than the others. I packed my belongings and my children and I took the train from Minneapolis to Detroit.

We lived with Aunt Ann for about four months. She helped me find an apartment, and soon my family and I were independent. My fifteen-year-old sister came to live with me that summer as I was pregnant; she remained with us until she finished high school. At age twenty-five, I was mother to three small children and a teenager.

Aunt Ann and Uncle Ed lived in a nearby neighborhood. My mother and younger brothers and sisters were in Toledo. We spent holidays there. My family was there when I needed them but didn't smother me with attention.

Over the next twenty-some years, I learned to parent. I was a disciplinarian. My decisions and directions were followed without question by everyone who lived in my house, my sister and my children. However, the discipline was tempered by love. As I became more accustomed to my role, I relaxed my authority.

My sister grew up and moved. My children grew into adolescents. They challenged my authority. They fought with me to allow them to make some of their own decisions. I learned to discuss, even debate, the issues with them.

As my children grew into adulthood, the second generation aged. Gradually, I was called upon to minister to them. A lot of it had to do with my being a nurse. If anything medical came up, they called me. I found myself making short trips or long-distance telephone calls to talk with their physicians or nurses.

Reflective Observations

My years of parenting different people in my family changed me. Indeed, I impacted their lives, but the most significant growth was mine.

I learned that parenting is not being the "boss." Parenting is seeing each family member as an individual and responding appropriately to his needs.

As teenagers, they needed to be allowed to venture out into the world, to interact without me, and to make their own decisions. Reflecting on those times, I remember them as a royal battle for control. We all came out winners. I learned the art of give-and-take. I learned the importance of communication. While all of us were so busy, we mostly saw one another in passing. I put a communications book in the bathroom for us to write notes to one another. Sometimes, we were able to smooth out minor problems right there in the communications book. For larger problems, we had and still have family meetings. The latest family meeting was held at my daughter's house. Everyone was present, including her then future husband. The subject was her upcoming marriage.

As the teenagers were seizing control of their lives, the second generation was relinquishing some control. They trusted me to make some decisions for them.

Abstract Concepts

During my training as a nurse, I learned quite a bit about the importance of the function of the family. As a single parent, it was a source of concern that my family not become dysfunctional. I studied sociology and learned that the family normally performs certain tasks. The socialization function was most important to me. According to Horton and Hunt:

> One of the many ways in which the family social-
> izes the child is through providing models for the child
> to copy. He learns to be a man, a husband, and father

mainly through having lived in a family headed by a man, a husband and a father. Some socialization difficulties are encountered where such a model is missing and the child must rely upon the second-hand models he sees in other families or upon other relatives. There are no fully satisfactory substitutes for a mother and a father, although they need not be the biological parents. [4]

I think this observation may be more true for a nuclear family. In the extended families described previously, others move into the role model positions with little or no adverse effect.

With the growing numbers of single-parent families, I see this occurring on a regular basis. Often, mothers are teaching their sons to be fathers.

In addition to socialization, the family has an affectional function. I recognized the importance of affection in the family most poignantly in the "failure to thrive" babies in my nursing practice. These were the children who were not cuddled or loved. They lost weight, stopped interacting and sometimes died. Death is an extreme, but it is clear there is an innate need for affection in the human life. The family also has the role of protector:

> In all societies, the family offers some degree of physical, economic, and psychological protection to its members. In many societies, any attack upon a person is an attack upon his entire family, with all members bound to defend him or to avenge the injury. In many societies guilt and shame are equally shared by all family members. In most primitive societies, the family is an extended food sharing unit which starves or fattens together; as long as a man's extended relatives have food, he has no fear of hunger. [5]

Sociologists have long labeled single-parent families as dysfunctional merely because they lacked a mother and a father.

I disagree with this labeling. I feel that if the family performs the function of a family, it is quite simply "functional."

Active Experimentation/Application

There were many changes occurring. Too soon, my teenagers were adults. I believe I recognized it before they did. Again, I changed my style of parenting for them. This time, I had experience. I moved from decision-maker to support person.

Now, in retrospect, they can identify the change. My son, Del, dropped out of college at one point. I hired him as a full-time employee in my company. When his older sister graduated from college, he was "green with envy." All of a sudden, with no plans or preparation, he was back in college with no money and unemployed.

I didn't try to stop him. I told him it was his decision. It was a tough year for him. There were times when he couldn't pay his rent; he lost his car. I lent him money to pay rent and paid his car note a couple of times. I let him know that I was there if he needed me. He would never be cold or hungry. Then I clenched my teeth and stepped aside.

Later, the following year, Del said to me: "You knew I wasn't prepared to go back to college, didn't you?" When I replied "Yes," he asked me why I hadn't stopped him. Then I asked him if he would have listened. He smiled sheepishly and said, "No, I guess not."

Passing of Leadership

Each matriarch has her own style of leadership and her own way of passing the responsibility to the next one. This was apparent in my family.

Concrete Experience

Mr. Game's death initially caused Momma to assume the role. Gradually, the family, under Momma's influence, turned to Aunt Hannah for support and assistance. This year, I recognized the beginning of another change.

A sign of the first passage of the matriarchal responsibility was when Momma took me to Aunt Hannah instead of to my own mother when it was time for me to start school. Momma had evaluated both of her girls' living arrangements. My mother was married, had two other children; she was young, impetuous and frequently in trouble financially and maritally.

Hannah had not yet remarried. She had completed school and become a licensed beautician. She also had other income from renting a couple of rooms in her large house. Her sister Ann also lived with her and had landed a job as a typist for the government. Momma recognized them as mature, responsible people.

She also recognized herself as an aging woman. She had diabetes and high blood pressure. A dizzy spell had caused her to fall from the top of an escalator.

I don't believe she said to herself, or to anyone else, for that matter, "Hannah will take my place." Nor do I believe she thought of herself as the matriarch. She did what she thought best to take care of her family. She recognized no nuclear or extended family boundaries.

She saw that I needed to be in a stable home environment. Perhaps she even looked past that and knew that, when she couldn't take care of herself, she also would live with Hannah.

As the years passed, Aunt Hannah began to call her house "home" to all the family. Many of them did spend some time at her house: cousin Leanna, cousin Claudette, Junior, and McKinley. After Aunt Hannah remarried, she took in family members of her husband, nieces, nephews, and a brother. At one point, she even mothered three foster children.

During that time, Aunt Hannah and I were not as close as before. She was busy with her matriarchal duties and I, unknowingly, was busy gaining the experience needed to one day step into her shoes. Many times she came to the rescue of Uncle Bill or my mother, giving them money or taking them into her home when they needed shelter. I remember hearing once that she worked an extra job to earn enough money to pay my mother's house payment, keeping her from losing her home.

Aunt Hannah and I led parallel lives until my children were older and her health began to decline. In recent years, we have moved closer as I became more aware of the needs of the second generation.

Some remain from the second generation: my mother, Aunts Ann and Hannah, and Uncle Bill. Each of them except Bill has adult children and some (Ann and Bill) have living spouses. I am third in the birth order of the third generation and the first girl.

Last year, Bill pulled me aside and asked me to come to Cleveland to help him with his will. Bill and his wife, Tolise, have hypertension and uncontrolled diabetes. They both have recently had complications related to both diagnoses. I mentioned Bill's request to Aunt Hannah; she replied, "Hurry."

Last summer, I had spent three weeks with Aunt Hannah. She is near seventy, hypertensive, diabetic, has glaucoma, morbid obesity, and a history of stroke. We both were delighted to be in one another's company, taking care of one another.

Each day, she prepared dinner for me. I drove her shopping. We collaborated on redecorating her bathroom. On weekends, I cleaned house.

We talked. She gave me advice. I gave her advice. We talked about her decreasing mobility. We discussed our children and our grandchildren. We talked about love, my love for her, her love for me. I promised her that I would take care of her. Although I live in Michigan and she in Maryland, we are only a phone call away. I promised her that she would not have to go to a nursing home.

Reflective Observations

Aunt Hannah's treatment of me was more like that of a peer. For the first time in my life, she treated me like an adult. Both Uncle Bill and Aunt Hannah were giving me more responsibility. I went to the attorney's office with Uncle Bill and Aunt Tolise. Reflecting on that day, I can analyze some of the actions and reactions that occurred.

It was difficult for Uncle Bill to explain his actions to the attorney. The four of us sat there in the attorney's office: Uncle

Bill, Aunt Tolise, my son, David, and I. The attorney wanted to know why Uncle Bill wanted to leave everything to me.

"Do you have any children?" he asked. Uncle Bill and Aunt Tolise shook their heads "No." Their only child died years ago when she was four years old.

"Is Barbara your only niece?" the attorney queried further. They both looked at me. "How many nieces and nephews are there?" Uncle Bill asked me.

"Lots," I told the attorney.

"Why, then, are you leaving everything to this particular niece?"

Uncle Bill looked a little perplexed and at a loss for words. The lawyer told him that he needed to know, should there be any question from the others later on. However, none of us had ever thought about any one of the family members questioning Uncle Bill's decision.

To us, the family, it was so simple. There had been a nonverbal communication in the family years and years ago that I was the family advocate. Over the years, they called me for help. It wasn't all because I was a nurse; there were other health care professionals in the family now.

It was only natural for me to be there to talk to the lawyer for Uncle Bill and Aunt Tolise. Before we went into his office, Uncle Bill told me that he was concerned about my cousin Pat. "Pat makes foolish choices. You know, her Momma's dead...I want you to take care of her."

There was no need for further conversation. I understood. He knew I would do what he wanted and that Pat would always have a place to go—if not his house, then mine.

My family has begun to recognize me as a leader. It was their acts of recognition that brought me to the realization that I am the next matriarch. I was quite surprised when my older cousin traveled two hundred miles to see me for a few minutes while I was visiting in Maryland. Curtis is fifty years old. He has a wife and a son. We sat in Aunt Hannah's kitchen and chatted. It was he who brought up his drug problem. He told me what kinds of drugs he was "doing," the type of people he associated with, and about his long, drug-abusing weekends.

I told him how I felt about what he was doing. Halfway through our conversation, I noticed the look on his face. He was listening intently. We were no longer chatting. He was digesting what I was saying. At that moment, my six-foot, 200-pound cousin seemed like my child. He was sitting, shoulders drooped, face turned up to mine, waiting for me to tell him what to do.

I gave to him what all mothers have to offer: my love, my support and my honest opinion.

Abstract Concepts

Our family has gone through several styles of leadership, starting with the authoritarian leadership of Momma to Betty, to a more group-centered leadership. The style has changed because of two main reasons: change of the matriarch and change of the followership.

According to Tubbs, there are three main types of followership: dependent, counter-dependent and independent.[6] Dependent followers are reluctant to act on their own initiative, respectful of the chain of command and unquestioning in following orders. Authoritarian or autocratic leadership produces a high level of dependent followership.

Tubbs describes the counter-dependent person:

> A second type of follower is the counter-dependent person. Counter-dependence is a type of behavior that is rebellious and anti-authoritarian. While the dependent personality is thought to result from overly punitive parents, the counter-dependent personality is thought to result from overly permissive parents. People who are used to doing things more or less their own way resent a leader or any authority figure who intervenes.[7]

Independent is the third type of followership. This person can either take over and lead or follow if he feels it more appropriate.

61

The first and second generation were dependent followers. In the third and fourth generation, I see all three types with an increase in independent followers in the fourth generation.

Active Experimentation/Application

When Uncle Bill told me to come help him with his will, it made me focus on where he really is in his life. For the first time, I didn't see him as the dapper young man of my childhood. A great sadness came over me as I allowed the thought to sink in that he is going to die someday. In my sadness, I wrote this poem:

> I look at Uncle Bill,
> The hair is gray,
> The jowls are droopy,
> The eyes, not so bright,
> And, I say to myself,
> Hurry, Hurry.
>
> When we walk together,
> I must remind myself
> To slow down when
> I notice he's not keeping up,
> And, I say to myself,
> Hurry, Hurry.
>
> He remarks that
> His eyesight is failing.
> He shows me his swollen ankles,
> And he's not hearing well.
> And, I say to myself,
> Hurry, Hurry.
>
> Hurry and say
> What you need to say,
> Hurry and ask
> What you need to ask,

Hurry and do
What you need to do...

For Uncle Bill's body
Is saying to all
That Uncle Bill's soul
Must soon take flight
Hurry! Hurry!
HURRY.

I believe that I went into training to be the family matriarch when I was a child. I used to resent being the one always told to run errands, do special chores, to fetch and carry. I realize now that was my internship. They (the first and second generation) started by giving me small, simple tasks. Momma always sent me to get a cold glass of water for her. Momma made me run the tap, put ice cubes in the glass and then add the water.

Under the tutelage of an aunt and an uncle, I learned to cook, wash, and clean house. Soon, I was accompanying one or the other to the outside world: paying bills, shopping. Eventually, I went alone to do those things.

I learned my lessons well. My early experience taught me the function of the family. I learned to recognize the difference between the nuclear family and the extended one and to apply actively that knowledge in identifying an extended family in another culture. That knowledge and experience were instrumental in my being able to accept my son-in-law's Nigerian culture.

Moreover, I could form my own opinion regarding the effect single parenting has on a child. I have come to the conclusion that two parents are preferable, but a single parent can also raise an emotionally healthy child. Having the support system of an extended family certainly facilitates this function.

Finally, I learned the meaning of the matriarchy. To the Curry family, the matriarch serves the family as much as she leads. This type of leadership works in many of my other situations.

We are in the final years of the second generation and I gladly take my place as the family matriarch.

I see that I am needed.

63

Table 1
Social Support Systems in the Black Community — The Family

TYPE OF FAMILY	Household Head		Other Household Members		
	Husband & Wife	Single Parent	Children	Other Relatives	Non-Relatives
Nuclear Families					
I. Incipient	X				
II. Simple	X		X		
III. Attenuated		X	X		
Extended Families					
IV. Incipient	X			X	
V. Simple	X		X	X	
VI. Attenuated		X	X	X	
Augmented Families					
VII. Incipient Augmented	X				X
VIII. Incipient Extended Augmented	X			X	X
IX. Nuclear Augmented	X		X		X
X. Nuclear Extended Augmented	X		X	X	X
XI. Attentuated Augmented		X	X		X
XII. Attentuated Extended Augmented		X	X	X	X

Source: Andrew Billingsley, *Black Families in White America.* (Englewood Cliffs, NJ: Prentice-Hall, 1968.)

Parenting in two cultures:
an Indian-American experience

As a mother parenting children in India and then America, Anjali contrasts the two experiences and what each taught her.

Dealing With Sibling Rivalry

I have been a parent for the last thirty years of my life. It is an aspect of my life that I think about and analyze in retrospect now that my children are adults. When I first became a parent, "parenting" was a subject that I did not think about in a philosophical sense; it was a fact of life for a young couple living in a traditional culture which expected newlyweds to become parents within the first one or two years of marriage. Parenting is being seen in a very different light today. I often wonder about the choices that today's young women and men have to make regarding children. Vance Packard, in his book *Our Endangered Children Growing Up in a Changing World*, writes,

> A young woman at a Tulane University panel discussion on alternative lifestyles tentatively asked: "I just want to get married and have children. Is that still okay?" One of the more profound changes occurring in Western society in the late twentieth century is this change in attitudes toward family formation. Having a child has changed from being a part of the natural flow of life to an apprehensive act or an act of courage.[8]

I acquired the basic parenting skills at a very young age. In the Indian family, the elder sister is considered like a second mother to her younger brothers and sisters. Thus, from the time that I was nine or ten years old, I learned to bathe, dress and comfort my five younger brothers and sisters.

When I became a parent, I knew how to care for my children's needs, but I also became aware of the full responsibility I had for my children's future and well-being. My experience as a parent has been influenced by being a single parent for some time: I was a working mother, and I raised my two children to be hybrids of two cultures. In this paper I will discuss the topic of parenting under the following subtopics: dealing with sibling rivalry; working mother versus housewife; and changing cultures.

From the time my children were born, communicating with them was important to me. This meant more than just talking with the children. When they were babies, I touched them and held them as much as possible. I played with them, sang to them and made funny faces to see their reactions. A crying baby meant that the infant was communicating that he was uncomfortable and unhappy. Thus, I made sure, as much as possible, that my babies were clean, well-fed and comfortable. In my small family I encountered the question of sibling rivalry on only one or two occasions. It was that communication which I had with my children which helped smooth situations at such times.

Concrete Experience

It is only in the last ten to fifteen years that Indian women have been going to hospitals to have their babies. When I had my children, about ninety-five percent of the babies were born at home. I had both my children at home with a nurse-midwife in attendance. When my daughter was three years old, my son was born on an early morning in November. When my daughter awoke that morning, she found that instead of me taking care of her, her dad was doing so. After breakfast, my daughter came to take a look at her new baby brother. She stood far away from my bed and pushed herself against the wall. Despite my imploring, she stated that she would not come to me unless I threw the new baby away. For the next week, she was not happy about her little brother, but by two weeks she had accepted her baby brother and was actually proud to show him off.

Reflective Observations

When I saw my daughter's behavior, I was concerned about her feelings. My husband and I came from large families, where we were used to having siblings, as well as several cousins, compete for our parents' attention. In the general chaos of a large household, neither my parents nor I noticed or explored any feelings of sibling rivalry. Therefore, I was not prepared for the feelings of jealousy my daughter exhibited now.

As soon as the baby went to sleep, I decided to have a talk with my daughter. Even though I was a very young mother, I was aware that this was an emotional issue for my daughter, and I would have to take a psychological perspective in talking with her. I told her that I understood her feelings and that I loved her very much. I told her that my feelings for her did not change, and that I had enough love for both her and her brother. I wanted my daughter to have a positive approach towards her brother, so I told her that from now on she would always have a playmate and friend in her brother. Although my daughter was very young, my assurances did make a difference in her attitude. Within two days, she was willing to sit on the bed with a pillow in her lap and hold her new baby brother for a few minutes.

Abstract Concepts

In looking back on my approach to dealing with sibling rivalry, I realize that it was my culture which determined how I and many parents in India explain to children that a new baby is about to become a member of the family. In a traditional, conservative culture, sex and reproduction are taboo subjects which are rarely discussed. If these subjects need to be mentioned, it is usually with many euphemisms, and a direct approach is not taken.

Life is seen as being made up of birth, marriage, and death; these things take place in all families and therefore nothing needs to be said or explained. Despite this approach to life, problems like sibling rivalry do occur in traditional cultures. Such problems are basic to all societies:

> Sibling arguing has been with us since Cain and Abel. It is difficult to determine how it began or how to make it end. It can be a valuable and constructive learning experience, but it can also be cruel and destructive. [9]

> ...All children at times feel resentful of their younger siblings because they have to share their parents' time and attention. [10]

Living in a conservative culture, the method I used for dealing with sibling rivalry—giving limited explanation but providing a sense of security—worked. My children understood what I wanted them to understand. However, in a technologically advanced culture like America, I believe that my explanations would not be enough. Children need to have proper explanations for why certain things occur in life and how their parents feel about life events. I would offer children a more complete discussion of how a family grows in number through birth, and I would also talk about understanding feelings of jealousy and competition among siblings.

Active Experimentation

The message that I gave to my children was that they were brother and sister and they only had each other to love and care for as siblings. I noticed that it was the passage of time and how my children internalized this message which made them accept each other.

My working as a single parent with my children being left alone to look after one another also made them more supportive and tolerant of each other. Since my own children are grown up now, I do not see sibling rivalry; however, I notice how my neighbors and people in public places deal with this situation. One of my neighbors has two children, ages six and eight. Every time she takes them shopping the children fight about who will sit in the front seat with mom. Finally, the mother gets tired and yells at both of them to shut up, and both she and the children feel bad. Although I would not interfere in their family, if asked, my advice would be to let her children settle the matter themselves, and the next time she takes them anywhere she can state her expectation in advance. She can tell them that if they behave themselves, then she will get them a surprise. Kersey further notes:

> As a general rule, however, children's arguments will be resolved more quickly if parents stay out of them. By intervening, we deprive them of a valuable learning experience and imply that they are not able to handle the situation.[11]

Another bit of advice that I give to parents who ask me, and also the one I used with my daughter, was to give the oldest child special privileges to help the child to see that his place has very distinct benefits. It also helps to let the older child know that the younger child will look up to him some day and copy the things that the elder does.

Being A Working Mother and Housewife

These days it is common to say that a woman either works outside the home or inside the home. Some women who stay at home these days may feel slighted by the publicity that working women get. I had left my college education to get married and begin a family. Before I had my daughter, I taught in a small private school for some time. After my children were born, I spent time being a full-time mom. When my husband decided to seek further education in the United States, my two children and I stayed behind for five years. I became a single parent and a working parent to support my children and myself. When we immigrated to Michigan, I "changed hats" again and became a full-time mom until my children graduated from high school.

When my children began going to college, I started working and slowly rebuilding my education.

Concrete Experience

When I began teaching at St. Thomas High School, my son was three years old and my daughter six. For five years, my children and I lived alone. My children and I went through many changes during this period. When my husband first left, my son did not understand why Daddy had gone away. Every time I called him to eat his supper, he would stand on the porch, look outside, and tell me that he would eat when Daddy came home.

I soon realized that I had to be very organized as far as my time was concerned. I would like to describe my daily routine. The purpose of this is not to relay my "sob story," because I was happy with what I had to do. Yet I would like to explain that oftentimes single mothers who live in less technologically-advanced countries end up with added burdens. I would wake up early in the morning and make breakfast and sack lunches to carry, then I would wash and dress my children and myself, and we would walk to school about three miles away. In India there are no stipulations that children attend schools within the same neighborhood or within walking distance. There are also no school buses, so most children walk to the school they wish to attend. For me it was easier to take my children with me to the school where I was teaching.

Since I had no car or refrigerator or other modern appliances, I would make all meals from scratch. When school ended, the children and I would walk back and pick up groceries on the way home. Once home, I would cook dinner, help my children with homework, and do my paperwork before going to sleep. When summer came and the weather was very hot, I would hire a "tonga" (a horse-drawn buggy) for my children to ride back from school. I would use an umbrella in the hot sun and walk beside the tonga, since I could not afford to also ride.

Since no child care was available or affordable to me, I made arrangements with the principal of my school to have my son sit in the kindergarten class, although he was too young to be in

70

school all day. Often I would be in my classroom teaching, and I would turn around to see my little son standing behind me. My daughter was old enough to understand that she must stay in her classroom. There are just a few examples of my life as a single parent in India.

Reflective Observations

I can now say that it was not easy being a young, single, working mother. Out of the hardships we faced, my children and I developed a bond which at times is even difficult for my husband to understand. My husband pursued his ambitions from his own choice, and although I supported him wholeheartedly, I felt that the children and I were directly affected by my husband's choices. However, we had no voice of our own in his decision. My husband had his ups and downs adjusting to a new country and "making ends meet," but I felt he had only himself to think about on a day-to-day basis. On the other hand, I could not think about myself or pursue my interests, because two little lives were completely dependent on me for their physical and emotional needs. Since it took fifteen to twenty days for letters to arrive from America, I realized that I had to rely on myself. Prayer and the knowledge of God were a very significant positive influence on my mental outlook and everyday life.

My life in India as a single parent brought many challenges, but it also made me a self-reliant and capable person. My life as a housewife was basically one of dependence. When I immigrated to Michigan, I found myself in a new world. My children, now eight and eleven years old, became quickly involved in school activities. My husband had a job and his own activities and meetings. I spent most of my time alone. I occupied myself with housework and volunteer activities, but I missed working.

Abstract Concepts

The role of parents is very important during the early years when children are developing the basic foundations of their personalities. Harvard psychiatrist Alvin F. Poussaint has made

71

the generalization that when both parents work outside the home "frankly it interferes with the nurturing of the children."[12]

Recently, there has been much concern over how children are being brought up. Our society is changing at a very fast pace, and as the traditional family is breaking down the children are affected:

> Children under age three are of particular concern because they are relatively helpless and have attachment problems with parent figures; the way they are reared in those first years will significantly affect their social, intellectual, and verbal development.[13]

As more and more mothers work outside the home, I feel that this will have to be an important consideration in their decisions. In retrospect, I can say that my children needed me to be with them from birth until they started school. I think this is true for most children.

> A large number of preschool children today have mothers who at some point will take outside jobs. Presently, at least a fourth of America's infants and toddlers under age three have mothers who hold down some sort of an outside job; among all preschoolers, the mothers of almost half have jobs.[14]

These statistics reflect trends since the early 1980s. As we begin the 1990s, many women who are financially able are choosing to stay at home with their small children. There are many unanswered questions about child care; women and men are forming new attitudes towards the role of parenting.

Active Experimentation/Application

As a working parent, both the quantity and quality of time spent with my children were important to me. That was why I took my children everywhere with me. I was the type of mother who felt comfortable when I could see my small children before my eyes. When my children were little I made quality time for them by spending time telling them stories, reading with them, and doing puzzles and games. I took them to movies, plays and picnics. We also went to church for our emotional and spiritual well-being.

"Latchkey children" is a relatively new phenomenon. According to one source, there has been an "explosion in the number of children who spend at least part of every weekday without any adult supervision."[15] This issue has been of concern to me since unsupervised children face many dangers. I believe we must explore as many options as possible to provide care for our children. One such option is using the help of grandparents and other relatives:

> In most areas of the United States, the extended family with relatives in the home or nearby is long gone. New York child psychiatrist Arthur Kornhaber reports that only five percent of United States children see a grandparent regularly. And that is a shame, he contends, because grandparents are natural allies of children. When they are in regular contact they are an extra source of love and companionship.[16]

I had no child care available to me in India. However, I think a particularly good example of child care was a situation my daughter was involved in here. I now recommend it for older children. When my daughter was fourteen years old, a single working mother in the neighborhood asked my daughter if she would be willing to be a companion to her twelve-year-old daughter on some days when the mother had to be away. My daughter was paid to be a companion, but did not have full babysitting responsibilities. The other girl felt mature and responsible having a companion instead of a babysitter, and the mother felt more secure knowing that her child was not alone.

I know that due to financial needs it is not possible for some mothers today to be constantly with their children. If the choice has to be between quality time and quantity time, I think quality time is more important. However, I think an on-the-job mom must ask herself what sort of life she would enjoy were she eight or ten or twelve. She must tend to her children's care and not assume there is only one alternative to her care—to leave older children home alone. There are many arrangements which will make an older child happier and busier than to be left alone for many hours, even if they seem old enough. The central question to child care is "Would I like to be living like they are?"

The lessons I have gained from being a working mother and housewife, of communicating with my children, spending time with them, and working hard, can also be applied to young women today. Many women face similar challenges.

Meeting Challenges of Cultural Differences

I have already mentioned several examples of cultural differences in the preceding account. The main factor of cultural change was the very essence of living in an Old World culture and changing to a New World culture. I came from a society whose language, art and way of life have a history that is over two thousand years old. Parenting in itself did not change for me. What changed was dealing with some different conditions as my children grew up.

Concrete Experience

Upon first arriving in America, I wanted to keep my traditional ways as much as possible. My husband was very excited and wanted us to assimilate as soon as possible. He bought us new clothes, and we were introduced to eating cereal instead of homemade bread for breakfast as well as eating hot dogs and hamburgers for lunch or dinner. We began watching more television for entertainment and exercising less. Our lives became quite sedentary compared to how we lived before.

When my children became teenagers they were not allowed to date, but I encouraged them to make friends of the opposite sex. Dating was a form of courtship which was not acceptable in my

74

traditional culture, and I wanted my children to concentrate on their education before they began thinking of marriage.

I also found that clothes were more explicit here, but I continued to make dresses for my daughter and buy clothes for my children even when they were in college.

Reflective Observation

It was inevitable that we would change clothing, food, language and other activities. What took longer to change was the way I thought about myself and my children. There were many activities, such as dating, in which my children were not allowed to participate. I did not actually ask my children how they felt; I just expected them to follow my wishes. I continued to make clothes for my daughter that were acceptable to me, and I just assumed that she approved of them as much as I did. I am sure my children had their own desires, but they were very obedient and polite children, and they continued to accept what my husband and I did for them.

Abstract Concepts

What I realize now is that it was the time I spent with my children and the circumstances of our lives which made my children put up with following my guidelines and rules for daily living. It was not until my children were over twenty-five years old that they even began to question my methods of parenting. Due to my own fears of drugs, crime and violence in this society, I tended to be more protective of my children. I sheltered them from harm, but I also kept them from exploring and learning many new things which are a normal part of living here.

> Some values can only be learned through experience while other values are reinforced and solidified through experience. It is tempting to protect children or shelter them from things that are unpleasant or uncomfortable for them. The difficulty is that some values cannot be learned if parents are overprotective.

Children need to get hurt, to have bad experiences and unpleasant things happen, and to experience the negative consequences of their behavior. To be too protective postpones this necessary learning process.[17]

Active Experimentation/Application

My children are now grown up, but when I look back, there are a few things I would do differently. I would allow them more freedom and give them choices and alternatives instead of just voicing my own ideas and opinions.

Some parents may drive their children into doing what they do not want them to do in the first place through having too many restrictions. One of my co-workers had a daughter in high school who had been dating a boy whom the parents did not approve. He was unkempt and took drugs, and my co-worker had tried everything to break off the relationship, without any results. One day she told me about her situation. My advice to her was that for two weeks she and her husband act very nicely toward her daughter's boyfriend—invite him to dinner, take an interest in him, and act like he is the best thing in the world. My co-worker tried this to see her daughter's behavior. Pretty soon her daughter started to break off the relationship. Although the daughter did not say anything to her parents, her mother felt that behaving according to my advice may have made her daughter realize the good and bad points of the young man. Perhaps instead of seeing only one side of the picture, she realized that without her parents complaining to her all the time, she was free to make her own decisions and see the negative side of the individual.

In the 1990s, we are realizing the value of many things like respect for elders, teamwork, and the importance of family and children. These are intrinsic parts of my Indian culture. My children and I have learned to take the good qualities of each culture and combine them into a philosophy which has meaning for us and, for the most part, works in our lives.

A passage in *Sensitive Parenting* represents the essence of my philosophy of parenting:

Children need space and freedom to become what they were created to become—not what we might choose for them to be. We must remember that we cannot make a rose out of a carnation.[18]

In this paper I have described some aspects of my life as a parent. I realize now that I have been a good parent. I have put my children before me and tried to do my best for them. They have turned out to be good-natured and capable young adults, and I believe they will go far in their lives. The love which I have for them has been what was given to me by my father, a love which is unconditional.

America is truly a patchwork of many cultural traditions. As these two women's stories illustrate, family traditions from other lands are not always abandoned, but rather kept or adapted in a new form. Sometimes traditional ways of a particular culture are merely grafted on to mainstream American culture. In a time of accelerated change, some of the traditional cultures' ways may provide some helpful blendings to technologically-advanced countries such as America. Perhaps through the collective wisdom gleaned from different places, these family stories can assist in responding to present-day parenting dilemmas.

Adult Learning Through Life Experience
or
THINGS I WISH SOMEBODY HAD TOLD ME

—Although perhaps not as efficient or ideal as the nuclear family of America's twentieth century, there are many healthy family forms. Some may be configurations conducive to healthy childrearing in the 1990s.

—Protectiveness has its own set of liabilities. Balance is an essential ingredient in nurturing children to adulthood.

—We are all part of a given family culture, although this may be most apparent through examining the contrasts of a subculture within the United States or another nation's mainstream cultural traditions. Each small or large family has its own family culture as well.

Epilogue

Today's children are living a childhood of firsts. They are the first day-care generation; the first truly multicultural generation; the first generation to grow up in the electronic bubble, the environment defined by computers and new forms of television; the first post-sexual revolution generation; the first generation for which nature is more abstraction than reality; the first generation to grow up in new kinds of dispersed, deconcentrated cities, not quite urban, rural or suburban. [1]

With the many "firsts" of this generation of children, we feel parents are more perplexed than in earlier eras. Perhaps it is only the morass of advice and information, or perhaps it is an illusion created by the media's focus on the unusual, such as child abuse, and new labels for nearly every childhood condition.

With the level of change so exponential, parents can no longer strictly rely on successful past practices to ensure healthy children. Today's children are growing up within new family configurations and an awareness of a larger world context. It is impossible to protect children from the enticements, the pain and the atrocities of a world beyond their immediate neighborhood. However, despite many changes in a child's environment, there are also many constants. Children throughout the world need love, care, security, consistency, safety; they need someone who will act as an intense advocate and cheerleader.

The parents in this volume have illustrated such characteristics. They told of difficulties and discoveries in providing loving, consistently administered discipline. They hoped that such careful discipline would afford their children security, safety and, finally, a level of self-discipline and independence. For many who found themselves as single parents, stepparents or dual working parents, providing loving discipline was not easy. Yet they found ways to "take lemons and make lemonade," even though some papers on parenting of children convey a certain amount of resignation, regret, and a lingering question: "How better might we have done this?"

With America remaining the only industrialized country without a national family policy related to its children's care, it is no wonder there are strains and regrets for these middle-American parents and student writers. Parents who also must work and study have great demands put on their time. But these are people who are going for a long-term goal. Our studies show that one of their reasons for earning a B.A. degree, usually under stressful conditions, is so that their lives can be easier than those of their parents, 90% of whom had no higher education. Perhaps more important is that these are adult students who hope to make their children's lives easier. They are aware of the increased competitiveness and squeezing out of the middle class over the 1980s. They hope to leave the 1990s with more security than they had entering it. They are investing in the future, with faith, hope and love for their children and grandchildren.

We hope their learnings were illuminating and helpful, because they struggled mightily for what they have shared in this small volume. We end with a portion of an article by Andrew Vachss, novelist, attorney and leading authority on child abuse. He is recounting an illustrative tale in which there is an imaginary set of persons conversing.

What children are, more than anything else, is this: another chance for our flawed species to get it right.

"What is the difference between an elephant and an alligator?" the old man asked me. It wasn't a question. It was the way he taught. The way his ancestors have taught since the beginning of his tribe.

"One's a mammal, one's a reptile," I replied. "One lives on land and visits water, one lives in water and visits land. One is a flesh-eater, the other a vegetarian. Neither has natural enemies."

"But both are hunted, yes?"

"Yes, I see. The elephants for their ivory, the alligators for their hides. They have the same enemy—man."

"You do not see, I asked you the difference, not the similarity."

"I told you many differences."

"Yet you missed the essential one. The difference that separates them forever."

"Is this a riddle?"

"Not a riddle, not a mystery. A truth you can learn . . . if you listen."

"I'm listening."

"The baby alligator comes out of the egg a perfectly formed predator. It will not grow, it will only get larger, do you see? It learns nothing. From the moment of its birth, it fights to survive. If it succeeds, if it reaches full size, it hunts. At birth, it is 9 inches long. In adulthood, perhaps 9 feet. The difference can be measured. As a predator, it increases in competence, in skill. But, no matter what its fate, it will always be what it was born to be."

"I understand."

"Do you? Your work is with children. To work with children, you must know the child. The baby elephant cannot survive on its own. It needs nurturing, it needs protection. Without love, it dies. Depending on how it is raised, the baby elephant grows to be a work animal, a circus performer, a peaceful beast content to live in harmony. But some elephants grow up to be rogues, dangerous to man. Depending on how they are raised—that is the key. You see the difference now?"

"Yes."

"And so, ask yourself: Are the children of man alligators, doomed to what they will be from the moment of birth? Or are they elephants, fated to be nothing specific and capable of anything?"[2]

Well-nurtured children are foundational to a truly healthy nation. Each is a gift, a blessing, grace embodied.

Appendix A

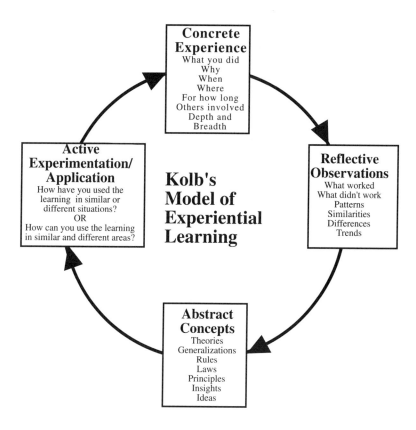

Kolb's Model of Experiential Learning

Concrete Experience
What you did
Why
When
Where
For how long
Others involved
Depth and Breadth

Reflective Observations
What worked
What didn't work
Patterns
Similarities
Differences
Trends

Abstract Concepts
Theories
Generalizations
Rules
Laws
Principles
Insights
Ideas

Active Experimentation/ Application
How have you used the learning in similar or different situations?
OR
How can you use the learning in similar and different areas?

Adapted from **D.A. Kolb and R. Fry, "Toward an Applied Theory of Experimental Learning," Cary Cooper, ed.** *Theories of Group Processes***, John Wiley and Sons, 1975.**

Appendix B

The model used by the students to demonstrate learning through actual experiences is Kolb's Model of Experiential Learning. David Kolb has integrated the learning models of Kurt Lewis, John Dewey, and Jean Piaget to develop his own learning theory.[1] Kolb's model is "a four-stage cycle involving four adaptive learning modes—concrete experience, reflective observations, abstract concepts, and active experimentation."[2]

"Concrete experience" addresses such questions as who, when, where, for how long. Readings, personal research and consulting with others are included in the term. In the "reflective observations" stage, the individual steps back from the experience and observes patterns, similarities, differences and what things worked or did not work. Then the individual would reflect on his or her observations.

As a result of the actual concrete experience and reflective observations, the individual draws conclusions and/or generalizations ("abstract concepts"). Often times this is backed up with theories presented by experts in the area.

Through "active experimentation" the individual applies the concepts and generalizations to similar and different settings to see if these concepts hold true.

Bibliography

Chapter One:
Balanced Discipline for Smooth Sailing

1. Bruno Bettelheim, "Punishment Vs. Discipline," *Atlantic*, November 1985, as quoted in Anne Eggebroten, "Sparing the Rod: Biblical Discipline and Parental Discipleship," *The Other Side*, April 1987, 27.
2. Barbara Oehlberg, "Love In Truth: Fixing the Problem Not the Blame," *The Other Side*, July/August 1988, 27.
3. Proverbs 3:12 (Douay).
4. Emily B. Visher and John S. Visher, *Stepfamilies: A Guide to Working With Stepparents and Stepchildren* (New York: Brunner/Mazel, 1979).
5. June Noble and William Noble, *How to Live With Other People's Children* (New York: Hawthorn Books, 1977), 26.
6. Research studies from Kelvin Seifert and Robert Hoffnung, *Child and Adolescent Development, 2nd edition,* (Boston: Houghton-Mifflin, 1991), 354-356.

Chapter Two:
From Lemons to Lemonade

1. Christopher Lasch, "The Crime of Quality Time," *NPQ (New Perspectives Quarterly)* 7 (Winter 1990): 45-49.
2. Jim Dugger, *Parenting: Ward and June Don't Live Here Anymore* (Shawnee Mission, Kan.: National Seminars Publications, 1989).
3. Anne W. Simon, *Stepchild in the Family* (New York: Odyssey Press, 1964).
4. Benjamin Spock, *Baby and Child Care* (London: Bodley Head, 1979).

Chapter Three:
Parenting Traditions Across Cultures

1. Thomas Sowell, *Ethnic America: A History* (New York: Basic Books, 1981).

2. Andrew Billingsley, *Black Families in White America* (Englewood Cliffs, N.J.: Prentice-Hall, 1968), 15ff.

3. Paul B. Horton and Chester L. Hunt, *Sociology*, 6th ed. (New York: McGraw-Hill, 1984).

4. Ibid.

5. Ibid.

6. Stewart L. Tubbs, *A Systems Approach to Small Group Interaction*, 3rd ed. (New York: Random House, 1988).

7. Ibid.

8. Vance Packard, *Our Endangered Children: Growing Up in a Changing World* (Boston: Little, Brown and Company, 1983), 20.

9. Katharine C. Kersey, *Sensitive Parenting: From Infancy to Adulthood* (Washington, D.C.: Acropolis Books, 1983), 115.

10. Ibid., 151.

11. Ibid., 115.

12. Ibid., 112.

13. Ibid.

14. Ibid., 5.

15. "The Latchkey Children," *Newsweek*, 16 February 1981, 97.

16. Kersey, *Sensitive Parenting*, 71.

17. Gary A. Crow, *The Nurturing Family: Back-to-Basics Parenting* (Millbrae, Calif.: Celestial Arts, 1980), 103.

18. Kersey, *Sensitive Parenting*, 228.

Epilogue

1. Richard Louv, quoted in George Kaplan, "Suppose They Gave an Intergenerational Conflict and Nobody Came," *Phi Delta Kappan* 72 (May 1991): K7.

2. Andrew Vachss' novel *Sacrifice*, quoted in "If You Could Listen to a Child's Soul," *Parade Magazine*, 16 June 1991, 4-5.

Appendix B

1. David A. Kolb, *Experiential Learning: Experience as the Source of Learning and Development* (Englewood Cliffs, N.J.: Prentice-Hall, 1984), 20-25.

2. Ibid., 40.